DATES
FROM
HELL

(AND A FEW MOMENTS
MADE IN HEAVEN)

DATES FROM HELL

(AND A FEW MOMENTS
MADE IN HEAVEN)

BY
VICTORIA JACKSON
AND
MIKE HARRIS

CUMBERLAND HOUSE
NASHVILLE, TENNESSEE

Copyright © 1998 by Mike Harris and Victoria B. Jackson

Published by Cumberland House Publishing, Inc., 431 Harding
Industrial Drive, Nashville, Tennessee 37211.

Cover design by Bruce Gore, Gore Studio, Inc.
Interior design by Mary Sanford

Library of Congress Cataloging-in-Publication Data
Jackson, Victoria, 1955-
    Dates from hell : and a few moments made in heaven / by
Victoria Jackson and Mike Harris.
       p.   cm.
    ISBN 1-888952-86-5 (pbk. : alk. paper)
    1. Dating (Social customs)   I. Harris, Mike, 1948 Oct. 7-
II. Title.
HQ801.J227   1998
306.73–dc21
                                       98-33596
                                         CIP

Printed in the United States of America
1 2 3 4 5 6 7 8 — 04 03 02 01 00 99 98

This book is dedicated to all you courageous souls who live life on the edge of Dating's Front Line—and who were generous enough to share your dating nightmares with us and with thousands *(millions, surely?)* of readers around the world. To paraphrase Winston Churchill: "Never, never, never give up dating. Just keep sending us your stories."

And of course, we dedicate this book to Martha and Bill . . . the two special people who have filled *our* lives with "Moments Made in Heaven."

mike harris & victoria jackson

contents

acknowledgments

Our deepest heartfelt thanks to the people whose insight, encouragement, and ideas helped to bring this book to life. Special thanks to publisher Ron Pitkin for knowing a good thing when he saw it, and to editor Mary Sanford for making a good thing better.

the world's funniest tales of dating disasters, and why you simply must read them

Let's face it. Dating can be hell.

And funny.

You are about to enter a world of awful evenings, noxious nights, and woeful weekends. True, funny-awful stories from men and women across America and around the world. Blind dates, prom dates, first dates, and last dates. *Particularly* last dates. There's one horrendous, hilarious tale after another.

Hilarious? Yes. Because nothing is funnier than the truth. Especially when it involves the tangled misfortunes of others.

If you are still among the *significant-other impaired,* these stories will affirm that you're not alone out there on dating's front line. Yes, there are people who have been through even worse dating experiences than you have—and lived to tell the tale. And after you've read this book, you can feel confident that nothing that can happen to you could ever be as bad as this!

And if you've already found that *special someone,* this book is an absolute must read. Why? Because every page will remind you just how lucky you are to have said goodbye to all that. Feeling a twinge of *itchy-feet-itis?* Hey, just dive in anywhere—anywhere—between these covers, and you'll have a whole new appreciation for your own situation. Think of it as the dating version of "Scared Straight."

Yes, we know. Not every date was spawned in Hell. So in this book you'll also find a few "Moments Made in Heaven" that will renew your faith in human nature and romance. Well, maybe.

By the way, you'll notice that in some of the stories we use first names only (or pseudonyms), while in others we use both first and last names. That's because while some people gave us permission to reveal their true identity, others did not see the need to trumpet their shame to the world. Hey, we can respect that.

So strap yourself in and hold on tight. You're on a roller coaster that is about to plunge into the world's funniest *Dates From Hell (And a Few Moments Made in Heaven)!*

DATES
FROM
HELL

(AND A FEW MOMENTS
MADE IN HEAVEN)

BLIND DATES—YOU WOULD DO THAT TO A FRIEND?

👹 keep on truckin'

delia tells us that for seven years she lived the single life in New York, trapped in a seemingly endless stretch of dating rejects from the *Twilight Zone*. One particularly memorable event stands out from the rest because it happened on New Year's Eve.

Delia's best friend Brenda and her husband Jay had moved to the Poconos a few years earlier, and sometimes Delia would drive over and spend the weekend with them. One particular year, she accepted their invitation to spend New Year's weekend with them.

Jay was a tree surgeon and worked with a crew of about six local guys. Jay had a great idea, he said. He'd fix her up with Jim, one of the guys on his crew, and they could all go to the New Year's Eve party as a foursome.

Delia realizes now that, in fairness to Jay, she had never informed him of her dating requirements or preferences. Jay, apparently using a sophisticated screening process known only to him, figured that Jim was gainfully employed and showed up for work every day—and they got along pretty well—so he must be an okay guy for Delia.

Delia figured that a New Year's Eve party would be an acceptable forum for a blind date, because she would still have her friends there in case things didn't work out. But they never made it to the party. At least Jim didn't.

The guys had been working all day, and probably had stopped off for a few beers on the way home. Jay brought Jim home with him so Delia could meet him before the party, which seemed like a good idea at the time.

Delia noticed that Jim seemed a little quiet as they all sat around Jay and Brenda's kitchen table talking, but she didn't think too much of it at the time. Jim suggested that he and Delia should bring a bottle of champagne to the party, and they decided to go to the local liquor store to make their purchase.

"We'll have to go in my truck," said Jim. "I haven't been home from work yet."

Leaving Jay and Brenda behind, Delia followed Jim outside to his truck. Now, this wasn't some little pickup or a 4x4. This was a big ol' two-ton truck, complete with all the weird and funky-looking equipment that tree surgeons use.

The first hint that there was a problem was when Jim kept repeating himself. He kept asking Delia the same questions over and over, and he was beginning to slur his words. Delia was starting to get a little anxious, but she figured they'd buy the champagne and be back to Brenda and Jay's in fifteen minutes.

They didn't get back for three hours.

First, Jim insisted that they stop at a local bar for a drink. Delia objected because it was obvious Jim had had enough already, but she was overruled. Delia sighed. Oh well, she thought. A quick drink and we'll be back in half an hour.

Once in the bar, Jim continued to ask her the same questions he had already asked her in the truck, only louder. By now, Delia was getting impatient and worried. As Jim's loud voice began to attract attention, Delia added "annoyance" and "embarrassment" to the growing list of emotions she was experiencing.

They finally left the bar. As Delia clambered up into the cab, she heard the unmistakable sound of a zipper being pulled down. Jim was relieving himself on the tire of his own truck. He winked at her. "I'll bet you think I'm just trying to impress you," he slurred.

Oh, yes, Delia thought with clenched teeth. She was *very* impressed.

Once they were in the truck and on their way again, Delia noticed that they kept passing the same landmarks. And it was starting to get dark. She looked across at Jim who was peering blearily through the windshield.

"Jim, are you sure you know where the liquor store is?" she demanded.

"Yeah, yeah, sure I know," he replied, "I just can't find it at the moment."

As a stranger to the area, Delia had no idea where they were, and it dawned on her that she was pretty much at the mercy of a tipsy nitwit at the wheel of a two-ton truck. They found a liquor store at last. But by now, it had closed for the night. Great. Jim, of course, decided they should set off in search of another store, again ignoring Delia's protests.

Jim was weaving the truck all over the wintery two-lane mountain roads, taking corners on the wrong side of the road, and driving way too fast. Delia asked him to slow down. Then she *told* him to slow down. Finally, she *demanded* he slow down. She'd stopped feeling impatient, worried, annoyed, and embarrassed. Now she was simply really, *really* angry. She yelled at him to stop the truck, right now. Jim blinked at her with his mouth lolling open.

"Well, if you think you can do any better, *you* drive," he smirked.

"Dammit, I will!" said Delia. "Pull over! Pull over, I said!"

Jim looked pretty shocked, but he did pull over, stopping the truck on a hill before opening the door and jumping down. As he stumbled around the front of the truck, Delia looked out at the trees. That's odd, she thought. The trees are moving. No they're not . . . the *truck's* moving! Jim had failed to put on the brake and the truck was rolling backwards, gathering speed. Delia threw herself across to the driver's side and dove under the steering column, then she jammed the foot brake down with her hand while she fumbled for the emergency brake.

Jim was once again relieving himself against a nearby pine tree, so he had missed this little drama. Unsteadily, he pulled himself up into the passenger seat, blinking silently at Delia who was by now sitting behind the wheel. She had driven a stick shift before, but never a two-ton truck with multiple gears. But by now she was angry enough and determined enough that she felt neither fear nor hesitation. She let out the clutch and lurched the truck forward with a grinding of gears. Jim would probably need some transmission work after tonight, but she was past caring. And so was Jim, it seemed. He leaned over, puked noisily out the window, then slumped back unconscious and snoring.

After what seemed like an eternity, Delia finally spotted a landmark that looked familiar, and after a few false turns, was able to find her way back to Brenda and Jay's house.

She stomped into the house, threw the truck keys on the table, and told them she was not going anywhere that night if she had to be in the same room as Jim. As Brenda and Jay stared at her open-mouthed, Delia gave them a brief synopsis of the previous three hours. They all agreed it would not be in anyone's best interest to proceed with the "date."

Leaving Jim to sleep it off, Delia went to the party with Brenda and Jay anyway. But without a date, and without the champagne, disheveled, exhausted and emotionally drained, Delia spent the most miserable New Year's Eve of her life.

Ah, the romance of the Poconos in the winter!

Delia has put New York and the dating scene behind her. She lives with her husband and their young son in Deltona, Florida, where she rarely if ever encounters snowy mountain roads.

☩ a tall tale

"**S**he was tall, so tall she could look through the windows on the transom above the door. I'm six foot two, and she looked down on me, literally and figuratively." So said Jim when we asked him about his worst-ever date.

"Her height made her compensate by trying to be careful with her 'small talk,'" added Jim. "The result being no conversation."

So how—and why—did this date ever take place at all?

The event was the high school graduation dance. She was Valedictorian, and dateless. She couldn't go to the dance without an escort, decided her mother. What could be done? Of course! Call Mrs. Hayhurst! Her son Jim was tall. Surely he would be the ideal date. And so, like the participants in an arranged marriage in some foreign land, Jim and the Valedictorian were "matched" for the dance.

From the moment they met, they both knew it was a mistake. Awkward silences. Sweating palms. A clock that seemed to run backwards. They came to an agreement. As soon as her official duties were over, the date would be over. And so it was. The miserable evening—for both of them—ended almost before it began. Jim went home early, much to the alarm of his mother, no doubt.

In retrospect, would the Valedictorian have been better off without a date, rather than being stuck with Jim and a night of mutual misery? Yes, thinks Jim, she probably would have. And he knows for a fact that he certainly would have!

Jim Hayhurst, author of The Right Mountain Crew, *lives and works in Toronto, Ontario, Canada.*

♆ the night is young—not!

"**G**reta Gusto" (as she asked us to call her) wasn't afraid of going on blind dates. Just as well, really, because she was returning to her hometown after a seven-year absence, and she had lost track of just about everyone she knew. However, she did run into an old classmate and asked him to introduce her to some of his single friends. Hmm, thought the friend. How about Gary?

Within a week, Gary called Greta, who thought he sounded interesting over the phone, and they arranged to meet on Saturday night. How bad could it be? Greta was about to find out.

Saturday. The doorbell rang and Greta opened the door. She told us that, just this once, she wished she had had the courage to say, "Ain't no way," and close the door. There stood Gary in his gray polyester pants (too tight), his gray matching JC Penney sweater, and gray patent leather shoes so shiny you could see yourself in them. His hair, what there was of it anyway, was clown red, and his stomach was no longer a stomach but a tire belly, right around his middle.

Okay, okay, Greta told us. I know you shouldn't judge a book by its cover. But in Gary's case, the cover was the best part, as it turned out.

The only other person that Greta knew in town worked in a restaurant, and that just happened to be where they went for dinner. As luck would have it, her friend ended up as their waitress. Every time she passed their table, she would look from Gary to Greta and snicker. "Boy, she's the happiest waitress I've ever seen," remarked Gary. The more they talked, the more apparent it became, at least to Greta, that they didn't have anything in common.

After dinner, Gary drove her to a bar where they couldn't find a place to park, and from there to another bar where they couldn't find a place to sit. Figuring that the third time's a charm, Gary finally took her to a redneck bar where, claims Greta, the chief activity of the men inside seemed to be slugging down beers in ten seconds or less and then roaring with laughter as they slapped each other on the back.

The highlight of the evening came when one of the guys loaded up one side of a round table with full mugs of beer. To prove his ath-

The Night Is Young—Not!

letic prowess, he then slammed his fists down on the other side of the table, catapulting a couple of gallons of suds, the mugs, a few ashtrays, and the remaining munchies across the room. Guess where they landed. How'd you guess?

Way after midnight, soaked in stale beer and the remnants of broken pretzels, Greta finally persuaded Gary to take her home.

At 7:00 A.M. the next morning, Greta's matchmaking friend called to find out how the date went. "Don't ask!" was all that Greta could sputter before slamming down the phone. Maybe, she thought, the solitary life isn't so bad after all. . . .

"Greta" is, however, now married. Not to Gary (surprise!) but to a photojounalist, for whom she is business manager.

he's not with me, honest!

"**h**ello, darlin'!" His words echoed throughout the restaurant as if through a megaphone. Every head in the place swiveled around to see the source of the loud greeting. Cathy didn't have to swivel. The voice was coming from directly in front of her table. She thought of her friend who had arranged Cathy's blind date with a friend-of-a-friend. "I'll get you for this," she vowed silently to her absent friend as she surveyed the spectacle before her.

Her date had driven all the way from Texas to Tennessee for this rendezvous with Cathy. He seemed to be going for a J. R. from *Dallas* kind of look. Six foot six, around 375 pounds, an oversized Stetson hat, and a silver belt buckle that Cathy could have used as a mirror. He reminded her of someone she'd seen on television all right. But it wasn't J. R. More like pro-wrestling's One Man Gang. Or Bam-Bam Bigelow. No. Like both of them put together, only with a lower level of poise and refinement.

By now he'd swung a chair around backwards and was sitting astride it; chewing, drinking Jack Daniels, and hurling cuss words as if they were arrows of love.

No doubt "J. R." thought that his manly language would somehow woo Cathy. Impossible as it seemed, the steady flow of whiskey increased both the volume and frequency of his profanity. The other diners had little choice but to hear the details of J. R.'s lurid autobiography. He was so proud of his life story, as if the fact that he'd beaten up every cowboy from Texas to Wyoming would somehow win Cathy's heart.

When he started giving her his opinion of gays and minorities, still at top volume, Cathy wanted to hold up a large card, emblazoned with the words "HE'S NOT WITH ME!" She gathered up her purse and started to get up.

He leaned forward with a leer and a wink. "How 'bout a little kiss?"

Cathy was actually thinking that a root canal would be more tempting.

Undeterred, he went for his best line. "So tell me, darlin', what's it going to take for us to get together?"

Cathy didn't have to search hard for an answer. "Reincarnation!" she hissed and headed for the door.

Cathy decided, as she drove home through the dark streets, that if this Hubba Bubba was any indication of the life forms found in Texas, then here was one little filly who wasn't going.

Cathy Townsend lives in Tennessee and knows in her heart that there are many fine, polite young gentlemen living in Texas. She just sees no need to go there and prove it.

♅ faux pas de deux

Shari still has the graceful elegance of the ballet dancer she used to be. However, she has traded in her tutu for a PC in her new role as executive vice president of an art college in the South. But from time to time, as she sits at her desk reviewing applications from hopeful would-be students, she remembers how her love for ballet led to her first date. Which turned out to be her first Date From Hell.

Shari loved to dance, and by the time she was sixteen she was becoming an accomplished ballet dancer. Fortunately, she had the perfect figure for ballet. Tall, willowy, and full of poise. Watching her dance brought joy to everyone who saw her. Including one particular young man who was struck by the beauty that radiated from the stage whenever she performed.

The day after one of her performances, one of Shari's friends approached her, wearing the furtive grin of someone just bursting to blurt out a secret. "I know someone who wants to ask you out for a date!" she told Shari in a conspiratorial stage whisper.

Shari's friend went on to explain that this young man had seen her dance and really, really, *really* wanted to go out with her. What did he look like? Well, she didn't know him personally. He was a friend of a friend. But she knew he was athletic—played high school football, in fact—but he was "kinda shy, so he's never going to ask you out himself," confided the friend. Naturally, Shari was flattered and intrigued.

During the days that followed, the friend would have put Henry Kissinger to shame as she carried out her mission of shuttle diplomacy between Shari and the friend of the unknown admirer. Finally, it was agreed. They would go to a dance at the high school. He would pick Shari up at seven o'clock on Saturday evening.

Shari looked forward to Saturday night with excited anticipation. A date! Her *first* date!

Saturday night arrived at last. Shari was checking her hair in the mirror for the hundredth time when the doorbell rang. Running to the bay window in the front of the house, she carefully drew back the curtain to look upon her admirer for the first time.

Faux Pas de Deux

She gasped. He was short. At least a head shorter than she was. With a buzz-cut. And pimples. He looked so . . . so *young*. Not at all like the dream man she had pictured in her mind all week.

In a panic, she ran to the kitchen and told her dad that whatever happened, she could not, *would not* go out with that boy. But he was adamant. A date's a date, he told her. She had agreed to go out with the boy, and it wasn't fair to let him down now. And deep down Shari knew he was right. With a sigh of resignation, she headed toward the front door and opened it just as her date was reaching up to ring the doorbell again.

He smiled and looked toward the point where he expected her face to be. Then slowly he tilted his head back as his eyes traveled up to meet hers. He blinked as his smile faded. He said, "Umm . . . err . . ." But Shari knew he was thinking, "You didn't look that tall on the stage."

Finally, he gulped and said, "Hi. I'm Bill. Are you ready? The car's over here."

As they walked toward the street, Shari looked her companion up and down. Mainly down. "Car? You have a car?" He sure didn't look old enough to drive.

"Yes," said Bill. "Well, kinda. My dad'll drive us." It was then that Shari remembered that her daydream date had been driving a gleaming convertible. But this was reality. Bill politely held open the door to his father's station wagon, and soon they were on their way to the dance.

They entered the high school gymnasium, which was decorated for the occasion, and Shari looked around at the gyrating figures as her eyes became accustomed to the lowered lighting. She noticed that everyone was strangely dressed. Everyone except for her and Bill.

Then it struck her. "This is a *costume* dance?" she asked Bill.

"Oh yeah," he shrugged. "I forgot."

Shari looked down at the definitely non–costume party dress she was wearing. It certainly made her stand out from the crowd. Only, not in the way she had hoped. Well, at least there was music and dancing.

Of course, dancing was the love of Shari's life. However, the same could not be said for Bill. No, he told her, he didn't dance. Now maybe he didn't want to make their height difference any more obvious than it already was. And maybe be was intimidated by her dancing ability. Whatever the case, Shari and Bill spent the evening hardly speaking a word to each other and enduring the curious stares of their acquaintances.

Finally, mercifully, it was time to leave, and Bill's chauffeur-father drove them back to Shari's house. She and Bill each forced a polite smile, shook damp hands, and parted forever.

In the end, Shari had to admit that the evening was not a total loss. Because of her Date From Hell, she instituted a new rule for herself: She would never again agree to go out on a date with anyone until she had had a chance to see them up close. And our bet is that Bill made the very same rule.

Shari Fox is now married to a tall man who likes to dance. They have four children and live in the South.

🔱 by the book

Cheryl had a natural inclination to help others. She had always been that way. Even when she was a child, she was the one to whom the other kids would bring injured birds. "Cheryl will take care of it," they would say. When she was older, lost children would come up to her at the mall. Somehow, they knew that she was the person who would help them. At the office, co-workers would unburden their souls to Cheryl, pouring out their personal problems to her. She always gave them a sympathetic ear, some kind words, and perhaps even a practical suggestion or two. Yes, Cheryl had always been that way.

And so it was only natural that Sandy would approach Cheryl and ask for her help. Sandy said that her cousin, Reg, had recently relocated to Philadelphia and seemed kind of lonely. "My husband and I are the only people he knows here, so he comes over to see us pretty often," Sandy said, then added, almost to herself, "Usually at dinnertime, without warning."

Would Cheryl agree to go out on a blind date with Reg? Please? It would be wonderful for Reg to have a night out with a female companion, and it would give Sandy and her husband a guaranteed evening alone. Anyway, Cheryl and Reg might really hit it off. Cheryl doubted it. But she was unattached, and just as you'd expect given her nature, she agreed to the date.

It was quickly arranged, with Sandy as the go-between. Reg and Cheryl would meet at a local restaurant for dinner. No question of going Dutch. Reg would pay for everything, Sandy assured her.

Cheryl arrived at the restaurant a little past seven. She would have spotted Reg even if she hadn't been given a description by Sandy. Something about the thirty-something bespectacled man with the thinning hair, sitting alone and staring at his lap, said: "I am Reg."

Cheryl approached his booth. "Hi," she said, "I'm Cheryl."

Reg looked up with a start. His mouth opened and closed silently, and then he began feverishly fumbling with something in his lap, hidden by the edge of the white tablecloth. Finally he stood up and held out a limp, damp hand.

"Hello, yes," said Reg. "I'm, uh, I'm Rex. Pleased to, uh . . . yes."

Cheryl sat down across from Reg. She was puzzled. He called himself Rex, but Sandy had said his name was Reg. *And what had he been doing under the tablecloth just now?* But being Cheryl, she smiled encouragingly at her dinner date.

"I'm pleased to meet you, too . . . Rex," she said. "Forgive me, but I thought your name was Reg."

"*No!* No, it's not," he answered firmly. "My name is Rex, not Reg. I expect Sandy told you it was Reg. It isn't. It's Rex." He looked at Cheryl, blinked a couple of times, and his shoulders sagged a little. "Well, I *used to be* called Reg. But I read that . . ." he checked himself. "I decided that Rex was more me."

Cheryl wasn't so sure about that, but didn't allow her understanding smile to fade.

As soon as the waiter had taken their orders, "Rex" again began to fumble in his lap. He's doing it again, thought Cheryl. After a few seconds, he looked up. Putting his elbows on the table, he leaned across toward her with his chin thrust out and a fixed grimace on his face. The usually unflappable Cheryl was startled. It took her a couple of seconds to realize that Rex's facial expression was his version of a friendly smile. His face was only inches from hers, but somewhat lower, due to the stretch from his side of the table.

"So, tell me all about yourself," he said.

Cheryl collected her thoughts. She didn't want to be mean. (In fact, she couldn't if she tried.) But his fixed stare was a little off-putting. She began to tell Rex about her job. Rex nodded energetically. Suddenly, Rex reared back, stared down, and began his lap-fumbling act again. Not again! thought Cheryl. Her description of her career stumbled to a halt. After a few seconds of silence, Rex looked up at her.

"Well, go on," he said. "Please go on. It's fascinating."

As their entrées arrived, Rex resumed his forward-leaning, chin thrusting posture. Cheryl noticed that his shirt front was dangerously close to his plate of shrimp scampi. By now, Cheryl had exhausted the description of her job, and because Rex insisted on steering the conversation back to her, she had moved on to talking about her origins.

"I've lived in Philadelphia for ten years," she said.

"Ten years, yes," said Rex.

"Before that, I lived in Harrisburg,"

By the Book

"Harrisburg, right," Rex repeated.

This strange echo pattern continued for several minutes, until Cheryl began to wonder if she had somehow stepped through Alice's looking glass and was in some strange bizarre parallel world. Once again, Rex crouched over his lap and began fiddling with something below Cheryl's line of vision. Cheryl wasn't one to think the worst of anyone, but even she was beginning to wonder what Rex was fingering under the tablecloth.

He emerged again just as she was picking up her fork. He glanced at her hand and immediately picked up his own fork. She took a morsel of food and put it in her mouth. Rex looked at her and did the same. With a deep sigh, Cheryl put down her fork, and opened her mouth to speak. A look of panic crossed Rex's face. His own fork clattered to his plate as he began to grab at his lap once again. But Cheryl was too quick for him. Her hand flashed out and grasped Rex's arm in a firm, no-nonsense grip.

In an equally firm, no-nonsense voice, she said, "Now Reg! I mean, Rex! What on earth are you doing?"

A look of misery clouded Rex's face. Slowly, he drew his hand up from his lap. He was holding a small spiral bound notebook. He put it gingerly on the table. Cheryl raised her eyebrows encouragingly, and, like hundreds before him, Rex began to tell her his story.

He'd never had much luck with the opposite sex, he told her. So he'd sent away for a mail order guide that guaranteed success in romantic situations. It had only arrived a couple of days ago, he continued sadly, so he hadn't had time to learn all the "techniques." Glancing down at the notebook, he confessed that he'd flipped hurriedly through the course that morning and made some notes. But he couldn't remember those either, and had kept the notebook on his lap, so he could refer to it as he went along.

"Why were you staring at me like that?" asked Cheryl.

"The book said I should make eye-contact and lean forward to show how interested I am in what my date is saying," answered Rex. "And to keep smiling, so I'll seem more desirable."

"I have to tell you, Rex," confided Cheryl, as kindly as she could, "It was kind of creepy when you kept repeating my words, and doing everything I did."

"That's called . . . um, wait a minute . . . 'mirroring.' Yes, that's it," said Rex. "It makes you more attractive to your date, the book says."

Cheryl was beginning to wonder who exactly had written this book. And whether Rex could still get a refund and go back to being Reg, who surely had to be a whole lot less bizarre than his new persona. At least she hoped so.

Even for someone as understanding as Cheryl, this was turning out to be a terrible date. But at least it was nearly over. The waiter brought the check, and Rex put down his Visa card. Cheryl noted that the credit card company had not yet been informed of the new-style Rex. The card was in the name of "Reginald." She stood up.

"Thank you, Rex," she said. "This has been . . . interesting."

Rex jumped to his feet. "Wait!" he said. "Would you like . . ."

He paused, eyes up at the ceiling, tongue gripped between his teeth. To Cheryl, he seemed to be searching his memory. He snatched the notebook from the table and turned his back, feverishly thumbing through the pages. Finally, he turned around again, and fixing Cheryl with grimace-smile, began his speech again.

"Would you like to have breakfast with me tomorrow?" Without pausing for breath, he continued, "Should I call you, or just roll over and nudge you?"

Cheryl stared at him for a second in disbelief, then turned to leave without a word.

"Wait! Did I get it wrong?" she heard him call after her. "The book claims *that* one never fails! Wait! Wait, let me check it again. . . ."

But Cheryl had already left.

Cheryl still lives in Philadelphia, and continues to care for sick animals. She draws the line at dating them though.

⚕ a blind date

harold will never forget his first-ever blind date. Indeed, how could he . . . ? It happened his junior year of college. He was doing some tutoring in economics.

A good friend of his asked if he could add another student to his roster. Harold replied that, really, he could not, because he was fully booked and had too little time for his own work.

The friend pleaded with Harold. Please, just this one. Harold sighed and said, "Well, who is it you want me to tutor?" And his friend told him it was Barbara Bonn.

Barbara Bonn?! Harold almost fainted. Barbara Bonn was the head majorette in the university band, and she was absolutely gorgeous. He couldn't say "YES" fast enough.

At the appointed hour, Harold was waiting anxiously for Barbara Bonn when he heard a tap, tap, tap coming down the hall. Into the room stepped a young man with a white cane and dark glasses. "Is Harold Black here?" he asked.

"Yes, I'm here," replied Harold. "Who are you?"

"Bob Rabanne," the man answered. "I'm here for the Economics tutoring."

Harold was speechless. His blind date really was blind. And a man. Sadly, Harold never did get to tutor Barbara. But, on the bright side, he tells us, he and Bob became close friends once they ironed out the misunderstanding.

Dr. Harold Black is Professor and Head of the Department of Finance of the College of Business Administration, University of Tennessee, Knoxville, Tennessee.

back from the head—with a tail!

Elaine told us that she was cured of blind dating when she was six-teen years old. It was during the Vietnam War, and most of the eligible young men in Santa Fe, New Mexico, seemed to be somewhere else. They were either serving in the military overseas or in training at camps hundreds of miles from their hometowns.

Elaine's friend Barbara had a serious boyfriend she was just crazy about. According to Elaine, Barbara had already bought her Corningware and packed it in her Hope Chest—that's how you knew their relationship was serious. Barbara's boyfriend was coming home on leave from the navy boot camp where he was going through his first few months of training. He was going to bring a buddy home with him, and he asked Barbara if she could fix him up with a date.

Elaine's own boyfriend was away in the service, too, and they weren't too serious about their own relationship. When Barbara asked her if she'd like a date with a sailor, she readily agreed.

"We'll go to the drive-in movie," said Barbara. "We'll come and pick you up at seven."

At a few minutes past seven on Saturday, a car pulled up in front of Elaine's house. Barbara and her boyfriend were in the front seat, and another young man was in back. Barbara's boyfriend introduced him to Elaine. "Elaine, this is Jack. He's my best buddy. I know you're going to like him."

As soon as she got in to the car, Elaine noticed that Jack seemed a little unsteady. Her suspicions were confirmed when he popped open a jumbo-sized can of malt liquor—obviously not the first. He began to chug it as if he were in training for the world speed-drinking record.

Before too long, he was sloppy, rip-roaring drunk, and he was all over Elaine like an alcoholic octopus. With her knees pressed to her chest, Elaine spent the journey fending off his sweaty paws. Barbara and her beau continued to chatter away in the front seat, blissfully unaware of the continuing drama being played out behind them.

Within minutes of arriving at the show, the inevitable happened: Jack threw up. Luckily, he'd managed to open the car door and do it outside, which was a blessing, Elaine decided.

Back From the Head—With a Tail!

Jack tapped on the front window to get his friend's attention. "I gotta go to the head," he slurred. Elaine knew enough navy jargon to know that "head" was sailor talk for restroom, and she figured she would get some well-deserved rest while Jack was gone. Barbara's boyfriend looked at Jack and decided he'd better go too, in order to help him navigate safely there and back.

A few minutes later, Elaine and Barbara were sitting in the car and noticed the wind had picked up a little. Then, in the darkness, they saw their dates returning, and from a long way off it looked as if they were being followed by some ghostly apparition. It was white, high above their heads and moving from side to side.

When the two men got to the car, Elaine realized that there was a less than supernatural explanation for this ghostlike vision. Jack had at least twenty yards of toilet paper trailing from the back of his pants. Somehow, this "rear" admiral had managed to drag his paper tail, without breaking it, from the restroom through a field full of cars, with gusts of wind lifting it like a ghostly kite above his thick head.

This was no doubt far more entertaining than the movie for the hundreds of drive-in patrons who had witnessed Jack's unsteady progress.

Somehow, Jack managed to get into the car with the tail still attached to his pants. He slammed the door and slumped into a stupor with most of the roll still outside, bobbing back and forth, waving at them through the window, as car horns honked and headlights flashed all around them.

Elaine slowly slid down in her seat in embarrassment, as far away from Jack as possible, and vowed that this was her last blind date.

Elaine Spear lives in Santa Fe, New Mexico. She believes that Jack might have single-handedly started the decline of America's drive-in theaters.

for male readers only!

Hey guys, let's face it. Asking a woman to go out with you on a date can be pretty unnerving, right? You have to accept the fact that there's a strong chance she'll turn you down. If you're lucky, she'll smile and politely decline your invitation. If you're not, she'll shriek, "Ha! Not even in your dreams, elephant boy!" Either way, it's what we here at *Dates From Hell* call "rejection." And it's not pleasant.

So that's why guys are particularly liable to fall into that black hole known as *The Blind Date*. Why? Because someone you know has told you that they know a woman who is actually willing to go out with you. Never mind if the best they can come up with is that she's "interesting" and "has a great sense of humor." At least you won't have your ego crushed again, like Wile E. Coyote under a plummeting giant Acme "rejection" anvil. Your buddy assures you that his girlfriend's friend/sister/aunt/gynecologist expressed an interest in going out with you.

Whoa! Hold it, Jack.

Okay, so she wasn't seized by a fit of projectile vomiting at the mere mention of your name. That's a good start. But, if you want to avoid a miserable, mind-numbing evening (or evenings, or—God help you—a lifetime), take a moment to listen to your friends at *Dates From Hell*. We've been there. We know.

Tell your buddy to give your prospective date a copy of the Pre–Blind Date Questionnaire you'll find on the next page. Make a few extra copies for future use, just in case. Don't give it to her yourself, you fool! You want to evaluate the results scientifically and rationally. Use your brains, not your loins. Looks can be deceiving. She might look like Pamela Anderson but turn out to be more like Louie Anderson once you're on that date. And that's not what you want. At least it shouldn't be.

Following the questionnaire, you'll find our patented Pre–Blind Date Evaluation System to help you decide if this date is really worth the effort.

And if it isn't, maybe *you'll* get to reject *her* for a change.

PRE-BLIND DATE QUESTIONNAIRE

Before our date, please fill out this questionnaire, so that I may better evaluate our compatibility. Using a #2 pencil, please completely fill in (e.g. ●) the circle that most accurately represents your agreement or disagreement with the statement.

1. There are many better things to do than watch football on TV.

AGREE   ①   ②   ③   ④   ⑤   DISAGREE

2. Getting to look the way I want to takes a long time. An hour is *not* a long time.

AGREE   ①   ②   ③   ④   ⑤   DISAGREE

3. Shopping is better than sex.

AGREE   ①   ②   ③   ④   ⑤   DISAGREE

4. Lorena let that jerk John Bobbitt off too easy.

AGREE   ①   ②   ③   ④   ⑤   DISAGREE

5. I buy Midol in the large economy size.

AGREE   ①   ②   ③   ④   ⑤   DISAGREE

6. It is perfectly normal on a first date for a woman to talk at length about her former boyfriend(s)/husband(s).

AGREE   ①   ②   ③   ④   ⑤   DISAGREE

7. Daddy told me that there isn't a man alive who is good enough for his little princess.

AGREE   ①   ②   ③   ④   ⑤   DISAGREE

8. A man should have no further need for his noisy, vulgar friends if he is serious about a relationship.

AGREE   ①   ②   ③   ④   ⑤   DISAGREE

9. When girls talk about how a man's buns look in tight jeans it is perfectly all right, but when guys stare at girls in tight sweaters they are dirty-minded, sex-obsessed pigs.

AGREE   ①   ②   ③   ④   ⑤   DISAGREE

10. There are many better things to do than watch football on TV.

AGREE   ①   ②   ③   ④   ⑤   DISAGREE

YOUR NAME ———————————————————

YOUR PHONE NUMBER ————————————————

Thank you for taking the time to fill out this questionnaire. I am looking forward to meeting you (assuming that the results of this questionnaire indicate a suitable compatibility index.) Have a nice day.

EVALUATING THE QUESTIONNAIRE RESULTS

Okay, guys, time to add up the score on your potential blind date and determine scientifically if she will be (a) the gorgeous, sexy, charming creature you've always dreamed of, or (b) the miserable, whining psycho you usually end up dating

All you have to do is add up the numbers in each circle that your potential date has filled in. Oh, and a few last minute qualifiers:

- Add five (5) points if you have reason to believe she has ever appeared on the Jerry Springer show.
- Add five (5) points if the applicant was recommended by your mother. (Add 50 points if the applicant *is* your mother.)

(And YES, Number 10 is a trick question. We think an important issue like this one bears repeating.)

Scoring your potential date

45 AND UP:	You've *got* to be kidding. Surely even *you* aren't thinking of meeting this woman. Let's hope she doesn't know where you live. If she does, move.
35–44:	You saw *Basic Instinct*? 'Nuff said.
20–34:	Well, this woman might be a possibility, if you're desperate for a one-time date. Such as picking up your Nobel prize in Oslo. Take separate airplanes.
13–19:	Now you're talking! Call her now before some other guy gets there first.
10–12:	She's lying, of course. But unless you happen to be Fabio, you're not exactly sitting pretty with your dance card all filled up. And let's face it: *you'd* have lied too, if she'd given you one of these things to fill out. You're perfect for each other.

for female readers only!

Ladies, how many times have you gone on a blind date and spent the entire evening wishing to God that you had realized what a total 100% dyed-in-the-wool jerk this guy was BEFORE you agreed to go out with him?

Lots of times, right? *Like, every time,* did we hear you say?

Well, this need never happen to you again, because now you can find out if he's Mr. Wonderful or the Creature From the Black Lagoon before you even get within sniffing distance of his rotten breath.

Here's how it works: When your "friend" says she has this great guy you should meet, reach for the handy Pre–Blind Date Questionnaire you'll find on the next page. Make a copy of it (in fact, make hundreds of copies; you'll need them) and have your friend pass it on to your prospective date. Do not—repeat, do NOT—attempt to give this to him yourself. The whole point is to form an objective opinion before you lay eyes on the jerk . . . uh . . . guy. Remember, handsome Doctor Jekyll was hiding Mister Hyde.

Do we take care of you or what?

PRE-BLIND DATE QUESTIONNAIRE

Before our date, please fill out this questionnaire, so that I may better evaluate our compatibility. Using a #2 pencil, please completely fill in (e.g. ●) the circle that most accurately represents your agreement or disagreement with the statement.

1. When I was a teenager, I spent many hours in my room alone.

AGREE ① ② ③ ④ ⑤ DISAGREE

2. Like everyone else, I sometimes suffer from embarrassing compulsions, but I manage to conceal them.

AGREE ① ② ③ ④ ⑤ DISAGREE

3. It is not necessary to look at a map for me to know where we are going.

AGREE ① ② ③ ④ ⑤ DISAGREE

4. Loud belching can be really funny.

AGREE ① ② ③ ④ ⑤ DISAGREE

5. T-shirt, baseball cap and cut-offs are perfectly okay to wear on any dinner date.

AGREE ① ② ③ ④ ⑤ DISAGREE

6. Employers have better things to do with their time than conducting random drug tests.

AGREE ① ② ③ ④ ⑤ DISAGREE

7. I can think more clearly after several drinks.

AGREE ① ② ③ ④ ⑤ DISAGREE

8. Women are secretly stimulated by crude remarks about their breasts.

AGREE ① ② ③ ④ ⑤ DISAGREE

9. I hold the remote control because I know what we want to watch.

AGREE ① ② ③ ④ ⑤ DISAGREE

10. My doctors seem to think that I am no longer a threat to society.

AGREE ① ② ③ ④ ⑤ DISAGREE

YOUR NAME _____

YOUR PHONE NUMBER _____

Thank you for taking the time to fill out this questionnaire. I will be in contact with you if the results indicate an acceptable degree of compatibility. Do *not*, under any circumstances, attempt to contact me. *Is that clear?* Yes. _____ (Your initials here)

EVALUATING THE QUESTIONNAIRE RESULTS

All right ladies, time to add up the score on your potential blind date, and determine scientifically if (a) he is the man you've been searching for, or (b) he's more likely the man that several state and federal agencies are searching for.

All you have to do is add up the numbers in each circle that your potential date has filled in. Oh, and a few last minute qualifiers:

- Add five (5) points if the completed questionnaire appears to be spattered with blood or other bodily fluids.

- Add five (5) points if the completed questionnaire comes back to you in an envelope bearing the return address of a state penitentiary. (Add only 3 points for a county jail. Hey, we're all entitled to make a few mistakes.)

- Add ten (10) points if the applicant signs the questionaire with three names (e.g. John Wayne Gacey, Lee Harvey Oswald, Long John Silver). Don't ask why. Just do it.

scoring your potential date

45 AND UP: He's a certifiable maniac, as well as a hopeless slob. Don't even think about dating him. And wash your hands after you have destroyed his questionnaire.

35–44: A brainless moron, and just being around him will make you feel queasy.

20–34: Hmm. A strong possibility here. But take a friend on the date with you. And a can of Mace.

13–19: He's either very cunning or very, very good. Oh, what the heck. Take a chance and go for it.

10–12: Get out of the way, honey! *We* want to marry *this* one!

DON'T GET PERSONAL

🔱 all you can eat

alan yawned. He wasn't used to dating this early. He checked his watch again. Seven o'clock. As in *seven* A.M. He looked around the half-empty restaurant. A couple of utility workers were helping themselves to more pancakes at the breakfast buffet. A salesman was drinking coffee while he checked through his call sheet.

Alan was beginning to wonder if this had been such a good idea. He had answered a personal ad in the newspaper. A couple of days later, he had gotten a call from "Sheila" who had said she liked his letter and thought they should meet. They had talked for a few minutes, and Sheila had a request. Was it okay if their first date were for breakfast, instead of dinner or drinks? It was unusual, but Alan agreed, assuming that Sheila wanted to be in a safe, public location for their first meeting. And that was how he came to be sitting in a restaurant booth at 7:00 A.M. He checked his watch again. Make that 7:05.

"Are you Alan?"

He looked up. The question had come from a pleasant-looking woman of about thirty. She was clutching a toddler to her hip with one hand. The other other hand was gripping the grubby paw of a child who looked to be about five. A slightly older boy was staring blankly at him while grasping a handful of his mother's skirt.

"Hello, I'm Sheila," she added as she slid into the booth across from Alan. She pulled the toddler and the five-year-old in with her. The eldest child climbed onto the red, upholstered bench alongside Alan.

"Sorry I'm late. I couldn't get a babysitter," Sheila added, somewhat unnecessarily.

Alan was looking at the kids, who were already beginning to squirm uncomfortably. He hadn't bargained on this. The waitress was putting glasses of ice water on the table. Sheila turned to her and issued orders with the skill of a real pro.

"We'll all have the breakfast buffet. Decaf for me, large OJs for the kids." Sheila raised her eyebrows at Alan. "Okay with you?"

"Uh . . . sure," he replied. But Sheila was already halfway out of the booth again.

"C'mon, kids," she called. "Let's grab some chow!"

Back in the booth, Sheila was telling Alan how hard it was to get babysitters, especially at this hour of the morning. "Nobody wants to help out single mothers these days," she said, then frowned at the boy sitting beside Alan. "Davey! Don't wipe that slice of bacon on Uncle Alan's jacket! You'll get hairs on it!"

Alan looked glumly at the grease and maple syrup smeared across the sleeve of his best jacket. Just then, the fretful toddler wriggled out of her mother's lap, made a lunge for her large glass of juice, and sent an orange tidal wave cascading across the table toward Alan's lap.

Suddenly, Sheila checked her watch. "Oh, look at the time!" she exclaimed. "I've got a job interview at eight."

Standing up, she reached over and plunked the sticky toddler in Alan's lap. Alan began to protest, but Sheila would have none of it. She was already picking up her purse and heading for the exit.

"Don't worry, I won't be long," she assured him. "Anyway, you told me on the phone that you liked kids. You *did* say that, you know. Be good for Uncle Alan, kids. Bye!"

The baby in his lap was now bawling at full volume. The boy beside him was kneeling on the seat making faces at the people in the next booth. The five-year-old had temporarily disappeared. How on earth did I get into this? thought Alan. He was already anxiously scanning the parking lot through the restaurant window. How long could a job interview take, anyway?

His thoughts were interrupted by the restaurant manager, who was holding the five-year-old by the collar. The child was clutching a handful of scrambled eggs. "Sir," said the manager through gritted teeth, "I must ask you not to let your children put their hands in the food on the buffet. The Health Department. . . ." His voice trailed off as he glared at the quagmire of mashed food, juice, and napkins on the table.

"They're not my—," Alan started to say, but the manager had already turned away, wiping his fingers on a handkerchief. Where was Sheila? This was turning into a nightmare.

But the nightmare was only just beginning. At ten o'clock, there was still no sign of Sheila. By now, Alan was fully occupied with frequent trips to the bathroom, which required him to take all three children each time, since he didn't dare leave two of them alone in the booth.

The restaurant staff cleared away the breakfast buffet and set up the lunch buffet. It was eleven A.M. Alan used his cellular phone to cancel the rest of his morning appointments. He had long since run out of ways to entertain this hyperactive brood. The manager seemed to be glaring at him relentlessly. Whenever Alan was concentrating on retrieving one child from a potentially disastrous situation, a crash or a howl would indicate that one of the others had gotten into something at the other end of the restaurant.

Noon came and went. Still no Sheila. Alan was seriously beginning to think that she had abandoned the children. He had a sudden vision of himself taking the kids back to his one-bedroom apartment. *No!* He shook his head to dispel the hideous thought. The eldest child was tugging his sleeve.

"We're hungry," he grumbled.

Alan sighed. He hoped they took credit cards at this restaurant. "All right, kids," He said. "Let's go up to the lunch buffet."

A half hour later, Alan was sitting with his head cradled miserably in his hands. His elbows were resting in puddles of soda, soup, half-chewed bologna, and macaroni cheese. He could barely hear the squeals and whoops anymore.

"Oh, good, you've already had lunch."

Alan looked up. It was Sheila, smiling benignly at her food-slathered family and their miserable babysitter. Alan was so pleased to see her that he instantly forgot the angry tirade that he had mentally prepared for her.

"I hope you were good for Uncle Alan," said Sheila, ushering the children from the booth. "Come on, now. It's time to go home."

Alan looked at Sheila. She was really quite good looking. And maybe he hadn't been fair to her. Surely, there must be a good reason for her absence. Perhaps a second date. . . ?

"Uh, Sheila, would you like to have dinner with me one night next week?" he asked, adding quickly, "Just the two of us."

"Oh, that's sweet of you," she smiled. "But I don't think so. We're not really compatible, are we?"

Alan gaped at her. Compatible? How would she know?

"Thanks for taking care of my kids," she called over her shoulder, as she herded her flock to the door.

Alan handed his Visa card to a very relieved waitress. "Babysitters aren't so hard to find," he thought. "You just put an an ad in the personals."

Alan lives in Baltimore. He doesn't do breakfast dates.

⚤ take your pick

"**L**et me tell you what *really* turns me on," said the breathy voice coming from the telephone pressed to Bob's ear.

Bob had responded to a personal ad. He didn't do that kind of thing very often, but there was something about her ad that had caught his attention. He was intrigued, fascinated. So he had mailed off his reply, addressed to "Advertiser, Box No. . . ." He had not really expected to hear from her, so it was a happy surprise when he picked up his ringing phone, and discovered that he was talking to "Advertiser."

As they talked, he determined that this was some special lady. She sounded sexy, playful, confident. And she had that breathy contralto voice that made Bob's ear tingle. They began to discuss their likes and dislikes, and that's when she made her revelation.

"Let me tell you what *really* turns me on," she said. "I love to see a man wearing tight, starched blue jeans and a crisp white shirt. That really *does it* for me," she added with a throaty chuckle.

"Uh-huh," said Bob, not knowing what else to say.

"So tell me, Bob. Do *you* own a pair of tight, starched blue jeans and a crisp white shirt?"

"Oh, yes," replied Bob, adding silently, *or I damn sure will by this afternoon.*

The voice purred its approval in Bob's ear. She wanted to meet him, she said. And she knew just the place. She named a trendy watering hole in town. They agreed that Thursday evening would be fine. By this point, Bob would have canceled heart surgery to meet this woman.

"Okay, Bob," she said, with a hint of promise in her voice. "Sit at the bar so I can find you. I'll be there about eight. And don't forget the blue jeans and white shirt! Bye."

"Wait! Hold on," said Bob, coming out of his reverie. "I don't even know your name. How will I know you?"

Again, the throaty chuckle. "Trust me. You'll know me." Click.

A few minutes before eight on Thursday evening, Bob pushed open the heavy wooden doors with the stained glass and leaded panes, and brushed aside some hanging ferns as he headed for the bar. He sat on a spare barstool and ordered a beer. As his eyes became accustomed to the darkness, he looked at his reflection in the large mirror behind the back bar. Yes, his spotless white shirt was indeed crisp. He glanced down at the freshly starched pair of tight

Take Your Pick

blue jeans he was wearing. Yes, everything was just as she'd request-
ed. This could turn out to be a really interesting evening.

Looking back up at the mirror, he noticed a strange coincidence.
The men sitting to his left and right were both wearing white shirts
too. This might cause some confusion, thought Bob. Better check
out their pants. As casually as possible, Bob leaned back on his stool
and glanced down to his left. Blue jeans. He looked to his right. Blue
jeans.

His eyes flicked back up to the mirror and met the nervous gaze
of the guy on his left. Then he noticed that the man on his right was
looking anxiously along the bar. Following his lead, Bob realized that
four more men sitting at the bar were all wearing crisp white shirts,
too. He leaned back. Yup. And tight blue jeans.

Suddenly his attention was caught by a new reflection in the mirror. An astonishingly beautiful woman had just entered the place.
She paused for a moment, until she was sure that every eye in the
room was on her. She began to approach the bar. Along with every
man sitting at the bar, Bob's eyes were riveted to her as she sashayed
toward them. She had long, straight, blonde hair and a *Baywatch* figure. She was wearing a tight tank top and a short skirt that revealed
legs that seemed to go on forever. Her strappy stiletto heels clicked
on the tile floor, then stopped. She stood at the bar, surveying the
line of male backs and buns, and the reflected faces of their respec-
tive owners.

The heel clicking resumed as she strolled slowly to one end of the
bar, then turned and made her leisurely way back. The eyes of every
man at the bar followed the progress of her reflection as she turned
again and raised the forefinger of her right hand. She walked a few
paces and stopped behind Bob. He could smell her musky perfume.
She reached out her hand and touched the shoulder of the man on
Bob's right.

"You."

Without another glance at Bob or his fellow losers, she turned and
strode toward the door. The lucky winner leaped from his stool and
ambled after her, his mouth hanging open like a dog sticking its head
out of the car window.

Bob felt crushed. None of the other men at the bar wanted to
meet each other's eyes, and the barman seemed to suddenly remember some limes that needed slicing urgently. Bob slid off his barstool

and made his way to the exit, trying to ignore the smirks of the other bar patrons. If he'd had a tail, it would have been between his legs as he pushed open the door.

It was the worst date he'd ever had. And he hadn't even gotten to see her face to face!

Bob now lives in Los Angeles, but he left his jeans in San Francisco.

ψ you like me? you really like me?

for most people, there is nothing more annoying than being with someone who is so full of their own self-importance that all they can do is go on and on about their wonderful achievements and how superior they are in every respect. Going on a date—particularly a first date—with someone like that can be downright torture. If it's ever happened to you, you've probably wished you could meet someone who was a little less full of themselves. Someone a little more modest about their talents and achievements. Kevin wished the same thing after dating a few self-obsessed women. But he reassessed that particular wish following his Date From Hell.

Kevin is a freelance artist and sculptor, as well as a sometime bartender. His bartending allowed him to meet a large number of interesting people, including single women, and he had formed a long-term relationship with one such woman. But that relationship had recently ended, and Kevin was spending more time in his studio and less time in social situations. He found himself without female company, and decided to try placing a personal ad in a local newspaper.

Kevin concentrated all his creativity into writing a witty and original ad. Within a few days, he had received three responses. He contacted Stacy, who had included her telephone number, and they had a nice conversation. They agreed to go to a movie together, arranging to meet first at a bar that was close to the theater.

At the appointed time, Kevin walked in and greeted a few friends he recognized, while scanning the room for someone who might fit the description Stacy had given him. He felt a touch on his arm and turned around.

"Are you Kevin? I'm Stacy."

They shook hands, and Kevin bought them both a drink, so they could talk for a while before the movie. It was immediately obvious to Kevin that Stacy didn't exactly match the way she had described herself on the phone, but still, he wasn't too disappointed.

"I'm sorry about the way I look," she blurted out. "I know I'm not real pretty. And you're so much better looking than you said on the phone."

Kevin was a little taken aback, and assured her that she was wrong and everything was okay. But Stacy wouldn't let it drop.

"I wouldn't blame you if you decided to end the date right now," she said.

Kevin was beginning to wonder if she had the right idea as she continued to tell him how unworthy she was to be his date. Was she really this down on herself, thought Kevin, or was she just fishing for compliments? He looked at his watch and stood up.

"Are you leaving?" asked the mournful Stacy. "You're leaving. I knew you would."

"No," replied Kevin. "*We're* leaving. We're going to a movie, remember?"

They got to the box office, and Stacy turned to him as he pulled out his wallet.

"Are you sure you don't want to run away?" she asked.

Holding up the two movie tickets as proof, Kevin replied—quite firmly—that he wasn't going to run away.

"Oh! I've annoyed you," Stacy sniffed. "I knew I would. I don't blame you for being upset."

Kevin ushered Stacy inside, assuring her that he wasn't upset, but she didn't seemed to be convinced and continued to recite a litany of her shortcomings. As the lights began to dim, Kevin looked sideways at his date. Despite her professing to the contrary, she was really quite pretty. As for her personality—well, he couldn't really say. All she'd talked about so far was how unattractive she was, and how unworthy she was to be on this date. He had sympathy for anyone who had such low self-esteem, but it really was putting a major damper on their date. He was grateful when the movie began, and they could both concentrate on something other than Stacy's inadequacies.

About halfway through the movie, Kevin whispered to Stacy that he had to go to the men's room. She looked at him and nodded with resignation. When he returned a few minutes later, she looked up in surprise.

"Oh! It's you," she whispered. "I figured you wouldn't come back."

It really was getting to be too much for Kevin, who was, by now, looking forward to the end of the movie and the date. From time to time, he'd be aware of Stacy looking at him and sighing or shaking her head. How could anyone be this insecure?

As they left the theater at the end of the movie, Kevin pulled out his keys. Stacy looked at them with a puzzled expression. She asked him what he was doing. He replied that he was going to drive her home, to save her taking the bus.

On the way, Stacy broke the silence. "Would you like to come in for a drink when we got to my apartment?

Kevin shook his head. "Thanks, but I have to return the car to my friend," he said. "It's not mine. I just borrowed it for this evening because my car is in the shop. I promised I'd take it back before midnight."

When he rolled to a stop outside her apartment building, Stacy again asked him to come in, and again Kevin declined the invitation. It wasn't an excuse. He really *did* have to return the vehicle. But frankly, he'd had just about enough of trying in vain to bolster her self-confidence. Stacy had one more question for him.

"I've never done this before, so I don't know what to say," she began. "I want to know if you'll call again, but I don't know if I should ask."

Kevin imagined spending another evening with Stacy, listening to an endless parade of her imperfections and inadequacies. It was not a pretty picture. But he didn't want to hurt her. Her self-esteem seemed low enough already. Whatever he said would create a major lose-lose situation. But he had to say something.

"Stacy, I've had a few blind dates," he said gently, searching for kind words. "I think it's best for each person to kind of digest the evening later, and go from there."

She looked at him for a second, and then her mood changed abruptly. Gone was the sad, pathetic, self-deprecating mousey little Stacy. In her place was an aggressive, assertive, lioness-like Stacy. Her eyes narrowed and her lips curled as she lifted her shoulders. It was like watching the transformation scene from a werewolf movie.

"I think," she snarled, "I've been digested!"

With that, Stacy sprang from the car and slammed the door, rattling all the windows. Kevin let the air out of his lungs with a whoosh, as the clicking of her heels receded into the darkness. His next personal ad, he thought. . . . How should he word it? ". . . *in search of self-confident young woman* . . ." He looked up as he heard her front door slam like a gunshot. ". . . *but not* too *self-confident.* . . ."

Kevin lives in San Anselmo, California. He might (or might not) answer your personal ad.

A Moment Made in Heaven . . .

Your Flight Has Been Delayed

Have you ever jogged through a crowded airport, carry-on luggage bumping against your leg, with one eye on your watch as the minutes tick down to departure time? And then you reach the gate just in time to hear the announcement: ". . . We apologize for the three-hour delay to flight number . . ."

What goes through your mind at a time like that? Anger? Dismay? Frustration?

Next time that happens to you, try to remember that maybe—just maybe—it could be the best thing that ever happened to you. If you don't believe us, just ask Denise from Franklin, Tennessee.

Denise tells us that in the summer of 1995, she knew she had to do something to change her lifestyle. She was mentally and emotionally drained. She was a 37-year-old corporate workaholic, and life had definitely lost its luster.

She decided that she was going to make a conscious effort to meet "nice" men. She went to all the right charity events and attended fundraisers. This resulted in a datebook filled with dates, but Denise was not overly smitten with any of them. Perhaps, she thought, she was destined never to meet the right man.

One night, Denise was at the Nashville airport waiting for a flight to Detroit. By chance, she spotted Mike, a guy she knew through work. She only knew him professionally, but she knew he was married, and therefore not a potential date.

As luck would have it, they discovered that they were both going to Detroit. And then came the announcement. The takeoff would be delayed for three hours. With nowhere to go and nothing else to do, Denise and Mike resigned themselves to airport limbo, and began to talk.

"So, what's new with you?" asked Mike.

And suddenly, for no good reason except maybe that someone had asked, Denise just began pouring her heart out. She went into detail about the woes of dating. Especially dating previously married men. How horrid it was, and how she wouldn't go there again. She might as well be a nun, she told Mike. Able to unburden herself at last, Denise went on about her dating miseries a little longer than she intended. Finally coming up for air, she asked what was new with Mike and his wife. Did they have any children?

Mike looked away and shook his head sadly. He and his wife were separated and in the process of a divorce. Denise was immediately embarrassed. And then, realizing there was the germ of attraction between them, regretted her comments, which had sent a pretty strong message: "Don't even think about dating me!"

Their evening together lasted about six hours total, what with the delay, the flight to Detroit, finding lost bags, and getting rental cars. And Denise enjoyed every minute of it. They talked about everything from Promise Keepers to the University of Michigan Wolverines. She knew she wanted to see him again, and deep down, she was thrilled that he would soon be "available."

Several weeks later, Denise had two tickets for a play. The tickets included dinner, and Denise was dateless. She hesitated for only a moment, then decided to call Mike and tell him about the tickets. Dutch treat of course. That would be safer all around. As it happened, Mike was out and she left a message on his voicemail. Later, she received his response on her voicemail: he'd be delighted to go.

They met for dinner and the show and both had a wonderful time. Denise told Mike during that evening that she was planning on taking her clients and staff to a special Christmas party at the Ryman Auditorium. Tickets for this event were very hard to come by, and, she told him, she needed an escort. Denise asked Mike to go with her.

"But I should tell you, there's a catch," she explained. "I'm going to dress up as Christmas Carol as a surprise for my staff. And my date has to go as Santa Claus!"

Mike looked at her with eyebrows raised. "So, what's the catch?" he asked.

The following Saturday, they dressed up for the evening and had the time of their lives! But it didn't end there. The costumes were rented for the entire weekend, they thought, so why not take advantage of them? They wore them to a "Towne Sing" at Mike's church on Sunday, and then they went on to a local hospital to hand out candy. By the end of the evening, Denise knew that this was definitely the man for her.

On July 4th, right after the grand finale of the fireworks display over the Cumberland River, Mike got down on one knee and proposed to Denise.

They were married in August in a wedding that, according to Denise, turned into a weekend-long celebration with family and friends from all over North America. Denise was 38 and had never been married. She has a sneaking feeling that many of the guests came just to see it really happen!

And so, if you are dateless—or shall we say "significant-other impaired"—take heart from Denise's story. Love came into her life when she least expected it. During a three-hour flight delay in an airport lounge.

Denise and Mike are now the proud parents of twin boys, Raymond and Zachary.

⚡ truth in advertising

osie had to admit that he sounded ideal. For the second or third time she was reading aloud from a personal ad. Not a personal ad in a magazine or a newspaper. This ad was staring back at her from her computer screen; Rosie was scrolling through a column of personals she had found on the Internet.

She ran through the highlights again, weighing the merits of each in her mind. *Fifty years old.* About the right age. *Financially stable.* Well, that was nice. *5' 11", 170 lbs.* Hmm, quite tall and slim. *Brown hair.* She liked brown-haired men. *Non-drinker, non-smoker.* Another plus. *Adventurous.* Rosie nodded. She was ready for a more adventurous life. *Divorced and ready to meet the world.* Well, that last bit could describe her own situation, thought Rosie.

Her marriage of thirty years had ended, and Rosie was finally ready to think about entering the dating arena again. But after more than three decades away from "all that," Rosie wasn't comfortable with singles' bars and the other traditional ways of meeting the opposite sex.

That modern miracle, the Internet, seemed the ideal solution. She understood computers, and it wasn't long before her explorations led her to this ad placed by "Jack."

She made up her mind. She would respond to Jack's ad. Her fingers darted across her computer keyboard, and soon her e-mail was on its way.

Jack quickly responded to Rosie's message. They realized that they lived relatively close to each other, and they arranged to meet at a Starbucks coffee shop downtown on the following Tuesday.

At the appointed time, Rosie was sitting at a small café table, stirring her coffee and looking expectantly at the door for someone who might resemble the description of her date, Jack.

"Are you Rosie?"

She looked up at the unkempt figure standing next to her table. Oh, no! Surely this couldn't be Jack! For a start, this person was certainly no more than 5' 8" tall, and he was at least fifty pounds heavier than the ad claimed. As for the brown hair, that was long gone. No, this *couldn't* be Jack!

He thrust a porky mitt in Rosie's direction. "Hi, I'm Jack."

In a mental haze, Rosie watched him pull up a chair and take the lid off his container of coffee. Jack began to tell her about his life. It was true that Jack was divorced. Three times, as it turned out. He hadn't been dating much recently, he said, as he'd just been released from a mental facility where he had been receiving treatment for severe anxiety. He spent most of his evenings at McDonald's because he was afraid to go home to his apartment alone. This wasn't going as well as Rosie had hoped.

Jack's eyes flicked left and right, and then he leaned in close across the table. He thought he should admit that, despite what it said in his ad, he did occasionally—just occasionally—have a smoke and a drink. Judging by the fumes in her face, Rodie decided that this had been just such an occasion.

So, Jack wanted to know, seeing as how they were getting along so well, would Rosie like to come back to his apartment? Rosie declined.

With a final sip of her coffee, she bid Jack farewell, and headed back home to her computer. On the way, she decided that she should have taken to heart something she'd once heard someone say: *"Truth in Advertising" is an oxymoron.*

Rosie Fuller lives in Oregon where she continues to surf the Internet but tries to avoid oxymorons—and other kinds of morons too.

⚵ no-frills dinner date

Y ou might think that Jared shouldn't ever be lonely again. Jared placed a personal ad in the local newspaper in Naples, Florida, and received eighty-four replies. Let's see: eighty-four Saturday nights. In theory, that should mean that Jared is "dated up" for a long time.

However, if you've ever placed an ad like Jared's you'll know that reality doesn't quite measure up to the theory.

So why did Jared run an ad in the first place? As he says, it's the 90s and the rules have changed. His corner of the world is dominated by women in most areas of retail and service businesses, while more and more men are finding themselves in the kitchen. And it's the men who are being asked out on dates and are the ones saying "no" to sex. Placing an ad was his way of getting back in the driver's seat, he said.

Jared kept the promise he'd made to himself, and called every one of the women who had responded to his ad. Of course, not all of these calls led to meetings, but a fair number did. Each meeting took place at a small outdoor coffee shop. Jared decided this was a good location, because not only do you have to pay your tab before you take your coffee outside, you're only a few feet away from your car in the parking lot just in case . . . well, just in case.

Many of the women described themselves as looking like one movie star or another. And in fairness, some of them did look the way some of the stars of the silent screen would look today. Over the next couple of weeks, Jared threw away a lot of cold coffee.

He remembers one woman in particular. In her letter, she said her name was Frilly. So when he called her, of course he had to ask.

"Where did the name Frilly come from?"

"My girlfriends gave it to me many years ago," she giggled. "It describes my underwear."

Well what do you say to that? Anyway, she sounded great on the phone. Good sense of humor, grown children, taking it easy. But she didn't want to meet for coffee. That was fine by Jared. He was actually getting a little sick of coffee. Frilly suggested that he come over to her place for dinner instead. But, she made it perfectly clear, there was to be *no sex* involved. That was fine by Jared. All he was looking for was a friend and a handshake goodnight.

He drove over to her condo, which was in an exclusive, gated community in the northeast of town. Jared arrived promptly at eight, and Frilly quickly put a vodka martini in his hand. Frankly, he was looking forward to dinner. He'd only grabbed a sandwich for lunch, and he was getting pretty hungry.

Frilly picked up her own glass, and Jared thought perhaps that it might not have been her first of the day. But she seemed very nice, both in personality and appearance, and Jared was pleasantly surprised to find that she actually did resemble the description she had furnished. And the tight pullover she was wearing revealed that she was certainly nicely endowed.

She led Jared outside where they sat beside her private swimming pool. Frilly noticed her glass was empty, and got up to fix herself a refill. Would Jared care to have his drink freshened, she wanted to know. Jared wouldn't. Drinking on an empty stomach wasn't a good idea, especially since he'd have to drive home later. In any case, he thought to himself, she'll be serving dinner soon.

Frilly returned to her chaise lounge a few moments later with ice cubes clinking in a brimming glass. They continued to talk, and Jared tried not to glance at his watch. His stomach was rumbling, and now he was *really* hungry.

Frilly fixed herself another drink. And another. Jared tried making a few hints about dinner. Maybe he'd misunderstood, and she was expecting him to take her out to dinner. No, she just waved off his hints with a smile and continued to drink. For two more hours.

Finally, she reclined back on her chaise lounge, and extended her arms out toward Jared. With her head tilted seductively to one side, she said, "Come here. Let's mess around!"

Jared looked at her sadly and sighed. Frilly didn't look quite as attractive as she had a couple of hours before. This was the woman who had stipulated, *No sex, come over for dinner.* Jared thought that he must be getting old. All he wanted at that moment was something to eat. Anything.

He stood up, shook her extended hand, and thanked her for a lovely evening, blaming a late meeting at the office for his sudden departure.

He took off for home, making an urgent detour to the drive-through window at Burger King. A Whopper had never looked so good.

Jared Wininger is editor of Pathways, a monthly magazine published in Naples, Florida. He really does enjoy a home-cooked meal, but a burger and fries will do.

BORDERLINE
CREEPY

𝌍 animal crackers

Studies show that bringing pets into institutions like retirement homes, psychiatric wards, and prisons can be an excellent way to calm the patients and inmates, and can help them relate more effectively with each other and the outside world. We're willing to bet that the authors of those studies have never interviewed Lacey or visited her, er . . . "friends."

All of this happened a few years ago when Lacey was in her teens. But, some events in our lives are hard to forget, however much we would like.

Lacey had agreed to go on a blind date, arranged by one of her friends. Ralph's a nice guy, she'd been told. Real interesting, kind of unusual. Looks like he's an artist or a musician. Perhaps Lacey was too inexperienced to spot the obvious warning signs in that description. Probably later in life, she would have put the kibosh on the date before it even started. But back then, she was dateless and a teenager, and had an offer for date. You bet she was going to go.

On Saturday evening, with her dad hovering behind her, Lacey opened the door to get her first glimpse of Ralph. The description she had been given seemed pretty accurate. He was tall and lanky with longish tangled hair, and he was wearing the universal uniform of jeans and a T-shirt.

He introduced himself, then immediately bent down and kissed Lacey on the lips.

"Just thought I'd get that over with," he told a surprised Lacey and her equally stunned dad.

Ralph took her out to the curb and helped her into his car, an old, mid-1950s "woody" station wagon, and they went out to dinner. Lacey doesn't remember much about the meal, or where they went, or what they talked about. Perhaps it was just not particularly memorable. Or perhaps it was obliterated from her mind by the scene that immediately followed it.

They went back to Ralph's apartment. He unlocked the door and pushed it open. Immediately, Lacey shrieked and jumped back. Staring back at them with a loopy grin was a completely naked man.

Animal Crackers

Naked, that is, except for a pair of socks.

"Oh, don't mind him," said Ralph with a dismissive wave. "That's just my roommate, Gunner. Say hello to Lacey, Gunner."

Gunner grinned unselfconsciously at Lacey, waved hi, then scuttled off into a bedroom. With her heart rate beginning to return to normal, Lacey stepped gingerly over the threshold. The apartment door opened directly into a scruffy living room.

Sitting on the sofa muttering to himself was a weird-looking character, totally absorbed in smoking a hookah. Pungent smoke curled from his nostrils and trailed lazily toward the ceiling. Lacey stared at him, still in shock.

"Oh, that's my other roommate, Jacky," Ralph explained. "He's uh, he's kind of busy right now. Let's go in the kitchen."

With a final glance at Jacky, who hadn't even acknowledged their presence, Lacey followed Ralph into the so-called "kitchen," a small, greasy room that was comprised of a cracked sink full of dirty dishes and a stove.

"Oh, wow! Great!" Ralph exclaimed enthusiastically. He had spotted a large bowl of strange-looking mushrooms on the stove. Reaching in, he grabbed a handful and shoved them into his mouth. Making "yummy" sounds while he munched, he offered the bowl to Lacey who wisely declined. She didn't know exactly what kind of mushrooms they were, but she had a pretty good idea.

She turned around, and for the second time in as many minutes, she screamed. In the corner, with whiskers twitching, were two very large rats.

"Hey, hey! Don't do that," said Ralph. "You'll scare them. That's Mickey and Minnie. They're my pets. Aren't you, guys?" He pulled from his pocket a roll that he'd taken from the restaurant and tossed it toward his rodent pals.

Lacey was pressed up against the wall, clutching her throat in one hand and the hem of her skirt in the other. She was beginning to hyperventilate. Just then, two large birds flew in from one of the bedrooms and, after circling Lacey's head for a few seconds, settled on the floor to battle it out with the rats for the roll. The birds were quail, Ralph explained, and they were Jacky's pets. Lacey was feeling a little dizzy by this time; she began to edge along the wall aiming to return to the living room. Even the semi-comatose Jacky was starting to look a lot more inviting to Lacey than the inhabitants of the kitchen.

With a feeling of relief, she made it back to the living room. Suddenly, she was aware of a slight movement out of the corner of her eye. She peered into the gloom. It must be the smell of those mushrooms, thought Lacey, or the smoke coming out of Jacky's hookah. She must be hallucinating. They had one of those long thin bean-bag tubes that you put under the door to keep out drafts. But it looked to Lacey like this one was moving. It couldn't be! But it was.

Slowly, it began to slither across the floor toward her. As it got closer, she could see its coal-black eyes and the forked tongue darting in and out of its mouth. With yet another scream, Lacey leaped up onto the sofa and scrambled over the catatonic form of Jacky, who was still puffing away blissfully. Attracted by the commotion, the rats and the birds had followed Lacey into the living room. The rats spotted the snake and decided to give it a wide berth. Which meant that they scurried over to Lacey's side of the room. The birds circled above, like Eyewitness News 'copters hovering over a highway crash.

By this time, Lacey was frantic. Clutching another handful of mushrooms, Ralph wandered in from the kitchen. The bedroom door opened and Gunner emerged to see what was up. Gunner had changed his clothes. That is to say, he'd taken off his socks.

Ralph looked puzzled. "What's the matter, Lacey?" he asked.

Watching the floor intently to be sure she didn't tread on anything furry, feathery or scaley, Lacey managed to make it across the room and out the door in three steps. Slamming the door on the loony zoo and its loonier keepers, she inhaled her first breath of air in a while that didn't consist of hookah smoke, funny-mushroom steam, or assorted animal crap.

If this is what you get with a blind date, she thought, you can keep it.

Before you invite Lacey Crawford to visit your home, we suggest you tell her what kind of house pets you own. Oh, and eighty-six the mushrooms.

🔱 good knight

a tall knight in shining armor, the sun glinting on the broadsword at his side as the gentle breeze ruffles the colorful plume high atop his gleaming helmet. A romantic vision indeed. But what happens when fantasy becomes reality? Is the real thing quite as enthralling? Maybe we should ask "Bonnie."

Bonnie met Ralph in a chat room on the Internet. Of course, meetings are somewhat different on the Net. Unlike bars, coffee houses, and restaurants, Internet chat rooms allow people from all over the world to "meet" without even laying eyes on one another.

Bonnie thought Ralph sounded like an interesting guy. They seemed to have a lot in common, with similar tastes in everything from movies to music. They even liked the same books and TV shows, including Star Trek.

At first, Bonnie thought of her relationship with Ralph as that of computerized pen pals. But as time passed, she began to think of him as more than just a casual acquaintance. He sent her a head-and-shoulders photo of himself, and Bonnie liked what she saw. Some of their correspondence concerned the subject of medieval knights. A few days later, Bonnie received a photo of Ralph dressed in a full suit of armor, complete with shoulder spikes. Okay, it seemed a little odd, but Bonnie figured Ralph was just following up on the mutual interest in the subject, and maybe trying just a little too hard.

Eventually, they arranged to meet. Seasoned surfers call it an F2F: "face to face."

When Bonnie entered the café where they were to meet, Ralph spotted her right away and stood up. Bonnie stopped dead in her tracks, her jaw hanging open.

Ralph was tall. Very tall. Close to seven feet tall, and well over three hundred pounds. He was dressed in black from head to toe, with a large medallion on a heavy chain around his neck. To say that Bonnie was in shock would be an understatement. The two snapshots had given her no indication of just how enormous he was. The other diners were staring at them by now, so Bonnie quickly shook hands with Ralph and sat down at a table with him.

After lunch, Ralph suggested they go to the mall across the street and walk around for a while. Ralph brought up the subject of their mutual interest in Star Trek. But Bonnie was about to find that, in Ralph's case, the interest was more like an obsession.

"I'm in a Star Trek fan club," he told her. "At the next convention, I'll be in a skit. I'll be wearing a kilt."

The sudden vision of that spectacle flashed through Bonnie's mind, and she swallowed hard to avoid giggling.

Ralph told her that his all-time greatest hero was William Shatner. Bonnie had already kind of guessed.

They spent a long afternoom going into every shop in the mall that had even a remote chance of carrying a Star Trek product. Or anything else dealing with science fiction, role-playing games, or skulls, which Bonnie discovered were his other three obsessions. By the end of the afternoon, he had completely recounted every scene from the latest Star Trek movie in precise detail, along with chunks of word-for-word dialogue. At least it saved her shelling out seven bucks at the local multiplex, thought Bonnie, but she had kind of wanted to see it for herself. Not any more.

Ralph then began an hour-long monologue on the benefits of having Captain Kirk as commander of your ship. This was turning into a very long and disappointing date for Bonnie.

you know it'll be a date from hell when . . .

The man says:

"Yes, I am married. But my wife doesn't understand me."

"I hope you're into the Retro Look. I just love to wear polyester leisure suits."

"Oh, gee! I seem to have left my wallet at home."

The woman says:

"I know they look bad, but they're just cold sores. Honestly."

"The guy staring at us? He's the guy I live with. Don't worry, we're just roommates, that's all."

"What are your feelings about people who've had trans-gender operations?"

Somehow, Bonnie allowed Ralph to persuade her to go back with him to his house. Proudly, he showed her what he called his "special" room. Black walls, black ceiling, black drapes. Groups of Star Trek action figures on a table. Large, full-size swords and daggers on display. This was definitely not a room where Bonnie felt at her most relaxed.

With a flourish, Ralph pulled aside a black cloth and revealed a computer where a grinning human skull—hopefully a replica—was perched on top of the monitor.

"This," said Ralph, "is where I sit when I am writing to you."

As that lovely image burned itself permanently into her mind, Bonnie mentioned the poster on the wall for the TV series *The Highlander.* The show is about immortal swordsmen who can only be killed by being beheaded by another Highlander.

"Oh, yes," replied Ralph slowly, as he took down a large sword from its display. He turned and looked deeply into Bonnie's eyes. "Didn't I tell you? I believe I am a Highlander."

All right, that's it, thought Bonnie. Time to end this before my head is rolling across the floor gathering dust bunnies. Unable to get Scotty to beam her up and out of this nightmare, she merely turned and left. Fast.

Next time you see Bonnie, we suggest you avoid telling her to "live long and prosper." Also, she's a little skittish around swords.

why can't a woman be more like a man?

even if Ken had never heard Rex Harrison singing "Why Can't a Woman Be More Like a Man?" from the movie *My Fair Lady*, there must have been times when the idea, at least, crossed his mind. Most men have wished, however fleetingly, that the ladies in their lives had more interest in . . . well, man stuff. But Ken learned that you should be careful what you wish for.

Ken's buddy Jim called him up and asked him if he'd like to double date. Jim's girlfriend had a roommate who wasn't seeing anyone special, so how about they make up a foursome and go to a ballgame? In that part of Georgia, "ballgame" could only mean one team: the Braves, and Ken was up for that!

Ken called Ginny, his date-to-be, and suggested they start out at a sports bar for a beer and some hot wings before going to the ballpark. Ginny enthusiastically agreed, saying that sounded like her idea of fun. Hmm, thought Ken. She sounds okay.

At the last minute Jim had to drop out due to an emergency, but he told Ken to go ahead and take Ginny to the game as planned. At the appointed time, Ken arrived at the apartment, and when Ginny opened the door, he was impressed with what he saw. "A knockout brunette," is how he described her. Nice figure, long hair, pretty smile. They asked Ginny's roommate if she wanted to tag along, but both were relieved when she declined their offer.

Outside the apartment building, Jim steered Ginny toward his car. Ginny took one look at his shiny vehicle and shook her head. "Nuh-uh," she said. "That thing'll get stolen. We're going to Atlanta, remember? We'll take mine. I'll drive."

There was no dissuading her, so Ken shrugged and agreed as Ginny jogged off to the other side of the building. He waited a few minutes, expecting to see her in a cute little Honda or some similarly feminine car. Then he heard a throaty rumble getting closer and turned to see a huge, gleaming Ford 4x4 heading toward him. Ginny reached over and pushed open the passenger door. "C'mon! Get in," she said.

Wow, thought Ken. This is my kind of woman.

She peeled the monster pickup out of the lot and hammered it into the traffic, tailgating all the smaller vehicles like a manic trucker. All the while, she kept up a constant commentary on her vehicle, using phrases that Ken thought only guys used. She told him what kind of cams and lifters she had, and how she fixed the spider gears in the differential. Stuff like that. He'd never met a woman he could relate to like this—someone who liked all these guy things. She seemed too good to be true. He actually pictured himself proposing to her! And he hardly even knew her!

By the time Ken had finished drooling over the truck, they were too late for an early dinner, so he suggested they go straight to the ballgame and eat later. No problem, said Ginny.

They had a great time together at the ballgame. Ginny matched Ken beer for beer, and demonstrated her skill at flicking popcorn at the people in front of them. She even bummed a cigar off Ken. Was there any interest they didn't share? The Braves won, encouraged, no doubt, by Ginny's enthusiastic hoots and whistles.

Before long they were at a table in the sports bar swapping jokes and having a great time while they waited for their order of wings— extra hot, the way they both liked them.

Then it happened: the first sign that the night was beginning to crumble. Ginny began to pick her nose. Not a discreet little wipe with the head turned, the way that ladies do it. Nope. This was a pick. A real excavation, right up to the knuckle. And all the while, she carried on with her story, while Ken alternately stared and glanced away. Now he knew how women felt when guys did something like that in front of them. Why did it make him feel so uncomfortable? After all, she was great in every other way. Loved trucks and beer and baseball and hot wings and smutty jokes—all those guy things. . . . He tried to make a weak joke about "fishing for the big one," hoping she'd get the hint. But she didn't.

Ken thought to himself, "Okay, I'd better work this out before I take her home to meet Mom and Dad."

By the time they had finished dinner it was well past midnight, and they clambered back into the truck, heading back to the apartment building in the suburbs. On the way, Ginny complained of gas from all those beers and wings. Shifting around on the bench seat, she managed to expel some of it, to her relief if not to Ken's. Sure, guys do that, but . . . but . . .

They reached Ginny's apartment to find a note from her roommate saying she would be out for the night. Since it was only a couple of hours before dawn, Ginny suggested that Ken sleep on the sofa until morning. He gratefully accepted and quickly dozed off, still unsure as to whether this was the woman for him. As he drifted off to sleep, he hoped there would be some kind of sign to help him make his decision.

The sign was not long in coming.

He awoke and rolled over. He slowly opened his eyes. The apartment was quite small, and there in the bathroom with the door open, only a few feet in front of him, was Ginny. She was sitting on the toilet, smoking a cigarette and reading the newspaper.

That's it, thought Ken. The End. I might as well be dating another guy. As he was leaving, Ginny told him to drop by the shop sometime. "The shop?" asked Ken, realizing that the one thing they hadn't discussed the previous night was where she worked. Right, Ginny told him, she worked at a Ford dealership.

"So, you're, uh, in accounting? Or the receptionist?" Ken inquired.

Ginny's brow creased. "No, of course not. I'm a mechanic!"

Ken pictured himself introducing her to his sisters. "This is my girlfriend. She's a mechanic." Nope. He couldn't do it. Sadly, he looked at this pretty young woman that, only hours before, he had been imagining as his wife. They actually had too much in common. Why can't a woman be more like a man? Hey, go ask Ken.

Ken Kirby still lives—and dates—in Georgia. He tells us that Ginny's review of their date soon got back to him: She thought he was nice but "too manly."

♆ no worries

Kate now lives in Ontario, Canada, but her tale of a less-than-heavenly date took place in her homeland of Australia.

She cannot exactly remember the details of how it came about, but somehow she had agreed to go out on a date with "Norm," the son of one of the local farmers. She does remember that there wasn't a huge spark between them, but he seemed okay, and she had nothing planned for Saturday night, so when he asked her out, she agreed to go.

Perhaps it would have been a good idea if Kate had nailed down exactly what it was that Norm had in mind for their Saturday date. She assumed they'd go out to the movies, or for something to eat. You know: normal date stuff. But apparently Norm was far from normal.

Kate was living with her parents at the time, and when Norm came to pick her up for the date, her dad gave the young man a slow inspection through narrowed fatherly eyes. He noticed Norm's wrinkled jeans and not-quite-laundered shirt, and pegged him for a dull, try-hard loser within seconds. Kate should have had such intuition.

"You be sure to have my daughter home by eleven-thirty, you understand?" said Dad, wagging a meaty finger at Norm.

Norm grinned and winked. "No worries, mate! C'mon Kate!"

They left Kate's scowling father on the doorstep and drove off in Norm's pickup truck. But instead of heading to the bright lights of town, Norm drove toward the sparsely inhabited scrubland that formed the edge of the Outback. Kate looked at Norm suspiciously.

"Where are we going?" she demanded.

"To grab some dinner," replied Norm, with another knowing wink. "No worries."

Before long, Norm spotted something off to the side of the road and slowed the pickup quietly to a stop. He reached behind the seat and pulled out a large flashlight. He handed it to Kate.

"Turn that on and point it over there," he ordered, indicating some bushes in the gloom about fifteen yards from the road.

Curiosity got the better of her, and Kate did as she was told. The beam of the flashlight picked out a large rabbit sitting frozen by the bushes.

"Awww," said Kate. Meanwhile, Norm was pulling something else from behind the seat. It was a shotgun. In a flash he pointed it out the window, and BLAM!

"AAAGH!!" yelled Kate. "You killed it!"

But Norm hardly heard her. He'd jumped out of the truck and was already picking up the dead body, which he tossed into the back of the truck.

Kate scowled at him when he got back in the car, but Norm just grinned at her, oblivious of the daggers darting at him from Kate's eyes. Before long, Norm stopped the pickup again. He pushed the

No Worries

flashlight at Kate, who, this time flat out refused to hold it. "No worries," shrugged Norm, who squinted into the darkness and again pulled the trigger. BLAM!

When Norm returned holding his latest victim by the ears, Kate confronted him. "All right, Norm. Where are we going?"

"Going? We're already here. I go out every Saturday night huntin' rabbits. You knew that when I asked you if you wanted to come with me, didn't you?"

"No," Kate told him, "I didn't know that."

"Ah, well," shrugged the unflappable Norm. "No worries."

By now, they were heading off-road, over rocks and gullies, chasing down rabbit after rabbit, with Kate's head bouncing off the seat back and the side window, as her nostrils filled with the scent of cordite, engine oil and dead bunny. The evening seemed interminable to Kate, who kept asking Norm what time it was. He'd always answer, "Not late."

Finally, when Kate asked him for the umpteenth time, Norm shone the flashlight on his watch. "It's about midnight," he told her.

"Aaagh! Midnight?! My dad's going to kill me!" Kate wailed. "No, wait; he's going to kill *you!*" Actually, that sounded pretty good.

Norm, of course, had the perfect answer: "No worries."

He turned the truck around and they bumped their way back to Kate's home, more than an hour and a half away. Not surprisingly, Kate's father had come outside when he heard the sound of the approaching truck, and was standing menacingly on the steps with his arms folded. Kate turned to Norm with her first smile of the night.

"*Now* I think it's time for you to worry," she winked at him.

As they got out of the truck, Norm reached into the back and rummaged through his night's "bag." Kate's father was striding out toward them, glaring at Norm. Before he even got to them, he started his angry greeting.

"It's about time! Do you realize how la——"

He trailed off as Norm swung around holding up two very large rabbits in each hand.

"These are for you," Norm said with a grin, swinging the furry offerings by their ears. "Hope you like rabbit stew!"

Kate's father stopped dead and looked from the rabbits to Norm and back to the rabbits. "Err . . . I . . . yes, we do," he stammered, his anger evaporating as he imagined his Sunday dinner. "Very much. Don't we, Kate?"

Kate stared open-mouthed at this instant bonding between the half-witted Norm and her father, who was by then reaching out to receive his tasty gifts.

Kate's father was all smiles as he took the rabbits. Remembering his manners, he looked over at Norm. "Er . . . it's kinda cold out here. Would you like to come inside for a cup of tea, Son?"

Kate glared at Norm, and clenched her teeth, hoping Norm would get the message. *"Son"?!*

Norm gave a lopsided grin. "Are you sure it's not too late?" he asked innocently.

Leaving a speechless Kate beside the pickup, her dad put his arm around Norm's shoulders and guided him toward the light spilling out of the open front door.

"Nah," said Dad. "No worries!"

Kate Aley says that her only consolation was that her father's short patience with dull, try-hard losers quickly overcame his appreciation of free bunnies.

STOMACH
TURNERS

✝ the good(?) night kiss

When Margaret was seventeen and growing up in Buxton, England, she couldn't help noticing some of the young men who hung around with her older brother, Mike. Most of Mike's buddies were two or three years older than she, and all seemed to be quite mature and worldly wise in Margaret's innocent eyes.

One fellow seemed particularly "dishy" to Margaret. His name was Dave, and Margaret tried to make sure that she was around whenever he came to visit Mike. Finally, Dave noticed Margaret. It wasn't that she'd been invisible, of course. But at last he seemed to see her as a potential date, not merely his friend's little sister.

Margaret's hard work paid off when Dave smiled at her one evening and asked her if she was busy the following Saturday night. Margaret cocked her head to one side and pursed her lips, looking into the middle distance through half-closed eyes, as if trying to visualize her calendar. No, she told him casually, after a few moments of mentally staring at a blank diary page titled "SATURDAY," no, it looked like she wasn't doing anything special. She held her breath and tried to look sophisticatedly bored.

"Want to go out with me? We could go the club. Go dancing, you know?"

Margaret pondered the question for a few seconds, then nodded. They set the time and said goodbye. Margaret managed—just—to make it to her bedroom before leaping in the air and shouting, "Yesssss!"

Next Saturday finally came, and to tell the truth, the date went very well. Dave was a good dancer. They seemed to have a lot in common and laughed at each other's jokes. The evening drew to a close, and Dave offered to walk Margaret home. Of course, she agreed. They walked through the dark Buxton streets, holding hands and talking about the club, and music, and mutual friends. As they approached her front door, Margaret wondered if Dave would want to kiss her goodnight. She certainly hoped so. After all, he was the dishiest boy she knew, and she *had* done everything possible to make a good impression. She had tried to project an air of maturity like those older women of nineteen or twenty that Dave knew. Now here they were at last, at her front door.

Their conversation petered out. Dave turned to face her. He gently put his hands on her shoulders and moved closer. *At last! This is it!* thought Margaret, as she gazed up at him. Dave's face was inches away from hers now. She parted her lips, and . . .

. . . *let out the loudest belch either of them had ever heard.*

They sprang apart. Dave filled with disgust, Margaret with mortified embarrassment. She clapped a hand to her mouth, mute with shame, her cheeks burning. Without a word, Dave took off, running down the street.

As luck would have it, Margaret's brother Mike chose this precise moment to open the front door. He looked at his crying, blushing sister, then at the figure scurrying off into the dark. He put two and two together and set off after the jerk who had tried to take advantage of his sister. Within a few strides, he dragged him to the ground. A tearful Margaret finally persuaded her brother that the man he was pummeling was his friend Dave, and that Dave was innocent of any wrongdoing.

As you might guess, Dave did not ask Margaret out again. And to make matters worse, Dave continued to hang out with Mike, so it was inevitable that Margaret was destined to see him again and again. And each time she saw him, she once again heard the echo of that terrible raucous belch that had come between her and her first true love.

Margaret Widlake and Dave were able to laugh at the "incident" in later years. Margaret is now married and she and her husband Terry own an English pub in Nashville, Tennessee.

⚓ feeling ill in illinois

One day, several years ago, Marilyn received a phone call from a man who said he had been given her name by a mutual friend. Could they meet? Perhaps go out on a date? He told her that he had recently left the seminary and moved to Chicago and, understandably, had few female acquaintances. Ever the adventuress, Marilyn agreed.

"Great," he said. "We'll go sailing on Lake Michigan with another couple." Now, this is where Marilyn should have said "No, absolutely not, forget it." Because she knows full well that she is a terrible sailor and liable to get seasick just from looking at a boat. But of course, she didn't say no, or this story would end right here.

Before sailing, he took her to dinner at a local deli that had a reputation for bad food and unsanitary surroundings. After her date ordered a large onion salad as his main course, Marilyn decided to give him a wide berth for the remainder of the evening.

Her date's onion breath was the least of her worries, as it turned out. As soon as the little boat began rocking and rolling on the choppy waters of Lake Michigan, a green-faced Marilyn became as sick as possible under the circumstances. Her gallant date totally ignored her woeful condition, chatting happily to the other couple as the yacht tossed and yawed across the water.

Here she was, retching noisily over the side with three complete strangers as observers. As a bonus, she was frozen numb, thanks to a sudden drop in temperature and a howling Chicago gale. Most men would probably head back to shore under these circumstances. Of course, this guy wasn't "most men."

Marilyn still remembers that it was several agonizing hours before they finally disembarked and her shaking legs gratefully found dry land. Her misery wasn't over yet, however. She crawled up the gangplank and lay down. Bad move. The world began to spin around her at breakneck speed. This sensation was, if anything, even worse than the one she had just survived.

When she could finally stand, her date drove her home in silence. He never called again, which was just as well. Later Marilyn heard

Feeling Ill in Illinois

from their mutual friend that he had returned to Washington, D.C., and re-entered the priesthood. Could the sight of Marilyn heaving over the side of a wave-tossed boat have had anything to do with his decision? She'll never know for sure.

Marilyn Kelly is president of Kelly Flour Company in Chicago, Illinois. She learned two things from this episode: first, trust her instincts, and second, never go sailing again.

⚔ a hard lesson

ravel broadens the mind, they tell us. Travel opens our eyes to the lives and cultures of other people. Travel takes us to faraway exotic lands. Places like San Francisco, for instance.

That's right, *San Francisco, California*. Because for Barry, who lives in Australia, San Francisco is an exotic faraway destination. When he reached his late teens, Barry realized that he had never had the opportunity to visit a foreign country. He'd seen movies and television shows, of course, and read novels set in exciting foreign lands. All of which increased his desire to see more of the world.

After hours of reading travel magazines and vacation brochures, Barry settled on San Francisco. It seemed to have all the benefits. Lots of things to do and see. No language problems. And a lot easier to get to from Australia than London, Paris, or New York.

Barry took a part-time job and saved carefully. It took a year or so, but eventually, he had enough for the airfare and a modest amount for lodging and spending money. The months went by, and before he knew it, he was sitting in a window seat on a Quantas airliner looking down on the City by the Bay.

He checked into a small family-run hotel and did all the things tourists do. He rode the cable cars. He climbed the hills. He went to Fisherman's Wharf.

On his second night in town, he visited a bar a few blocks from his hotel. His trip to the United States wouldn't be complete without drinking a Bud or two in a friendly neighborhood tavern. He walked inside, and after his eyes became accustomed to the darkness, he hitched himself up on a barstool and ordered a beer.

Almost immediately, he noticed a young woman at the other end of the bar. He caught his breath. She truly was the "American Dream"; the kind of woman he'd seen on American TV shows like *Dallas* and *Baywatch*. Acres of platinum hair, short skirt, and stockings covering legs that seemed to go up to her shoulder blades.

As Barry contemplated how to make his move, this vision of loveliness slid off her barstool and walked over to him. She smiled and began talking to him with a slow, resonant, breathy voice. Barry thought to himself, This country really is the land of opportunity.

They talked and had a couple of drinks. Barry began to realize that the close-up view was not quite as good as the long-range one. For a start, she had rather ugly hands. But Barry was young and flat-

women: top ten ways to ensure you have a date from hell

10. If he says, "Where would you like to go?" just say, "Oh, anywhere is fine."

9. Agree to meet him after his favorite bar closes at 2:00 A.M.

8. Go on a blind date with a guy who takes you to a Star Trek convention.

7. Go away on a three-day weekend hiking expedition with a guy, and wear your brand-new, very stiff, extra tough hiking boots for the very first time. And forget to bring your socks.

6. Forget until the last minute to call a babysitter. Give up after trying four or five; bring the kids along on the date.

5. The guy says he has to postpone the date until tomorrow, because this evening he has to go meet his parole officer. Say okay.

4. Agree to meet him at his house, because he says his mother has to give her approval before he can go out with you.

3. Agree to put his plastic baggie of white powder in your purse "just until we lose this cop that's following us."

2. Nod sympathetically when he says that it is important for his underwear to be pressed and starched, even if most people never see it.

And of course . . .

1. Go back to his place and don't bat an eye when he asks you to choose the French Maid's costume or the schoolgirl outfit. (Even if you're not so sure which one of you he thinks is going to wear it.)

tered by her attention. And, frankly, nobody else had given him a second glance.

After a while, she suggested they leave the bar, and about a block away, she guided him into a darkened doorway for a kiss. *What a find,* thought Barry. She certainly wasn't like the shy Australian girls he was used to. They began to kiss passionately, as she ran her hands over Barry's back and through his hair.

Suddenly, Barry was aware of something that shouldn't be there. It was a lump. A very large lump. It was pressing against his stomach. And it didn't belong to him.

Barry disentangled himself from his conquest. He stared at her in horror.

"You . . . *you're* not a woman!" he finally spluttered. "You're a . . . you're a . . ."

"She" rolled her eyes heavenwards. "Oh, please! Who were you expecting, Betty Grable?"

Barry stumbled backwards out of the doorway, wiping the lipstick from his face with the back of his hand. The kid from small town Australia barely knew such people existed. In a panic, he turned and ran.

He arrived back at his hotel in a frenzy. The elderly doorman could see that he was distressed and wanted to know if he'd been attacked or robbed. Barry blurted out his story. Shaking his head sadly, the doorman sat Barry down in the lobby with a hot cup of coffee, and explained a few facts of life. Particularly, those facts that applied to certain bars in San Francisco.

And Barry asked himself, "Why didn't I talk to this guy a few hours earlier?"

"Barry" is not his real name. He still lives in Australia, but now he's a little more worldly wise.

⚜ last dance

norma's worst-ever date took place deep in the heart of Texas, and, as big as the Lone Star State is, we don't think it is quite big enough for both Norma and her date, "Tex."

It was one of those evenings that started out with a lot of promise but quickly went downhill. However, we have a feeling that to this day Tex still doesn't realize where he went wrong.

On reflection, Norma thinks she might be partially to blame. After all, she could have said that she didn't dance. But that wouldn't have been true, because she loves to dance. Dance in high heels, that is,

Last Dance

not in boots. Boots? Yup. Tex was taking her to a country dance club. And that, Norma quickly discovered, is very different from a Country Club dance.

They arrived at the club and the music started. Tex immediately took her in his arms, and they began to dance to a slow country tune. Tex was a sweet and very attentive guy. He didn't take his arm away from her shoulder, and every few moments he would lean in toward her, nuzzling her neck and hair.

As the music ended, Tex stepped back and Norma noticed that there was a paper cup clutched in the hand that was attached to that attentive arm. And in the cup was a sloppy mess of dark brown liquid. Cola? Coffee? Shucks, no. This was Texas, remember? Oh, yes, the cup that Tex had lovingly cradled next to Norma's ear contained an appetizing mixture of saliva and tobacco juice!

A quick check in the ladies' room mirror confirmed Norma's suspicion. The back of her white silk blouse was spattered with an interesting pattern of brown dribbles, thanks to Tex's not-so-good aim.

A tight-lipped Norma informed Tex that the date was over, right now, and it was time to leave. It may have been the first dance of the evening, but it was *their* last dance, ever.

After that night, whenever Norma was asked to go dancing, she made certain that boots were not required. Likewise paper cups.

Norma Gerson passed away shortly after telling us this story. She was an Emmy award-winning makeup artist, and will be sadly missed.

CAUGHT IN
THE ACT

⚱ mustang by moonlight

If there is one thing Graeme has always loved, it is a classic American automobile. Perhaps his passion is fueled by the fact that he lives a long way from Detroit. In fact, Graeme lives in Tasmania, the beautiful island off the south coast of mainland Australia.

He's never missed an opportunity for a close-up look at a '57 Chevy or a Cadillac Eldorado whenever one has crossed his path. But his favorite of all was a classic Ford Mustang, and it was one of those growling beauties that played a part in an evening that he will not soon forget.

Graeme was on vacation with his wife and children at a resort area in Tasmania. The icing on the cake was the beautiful red Mustang that he had managed to rent from a company that specialized in a small fleet of classic American cars. It cost more than the usual rental car, but Graeme figured he was on vacation, and the extra charge was well worth it.

He made good use of the car that week. He drove the family pretty much everywhere in it, even when they could just as easily have walked. Graeme wanted to make the most of every minute that he had with the car.

Their week's vacation was coming to an end. And much as they enjoyed being with their children, Graeme and his wife wanted some time just to be with each other. Graeme talked to a manager at the hotel and explained the situation. After a few minutes and a couple of phone calls, the manager had arranged for a babysitter to take care of the kids.

An evening of romance began with a delightful candlelit dinner for two at an oceanside restaurant. It continued with a stroll to the casino for a few spins of the roulette wheel. Graeme was beginning to feel like James Bond.

It was a beautiful evening. The stars were twinkling and a full moon shone in the clear night sky. They could hear the surf crashing on the beach and feel the cool breeze waft in from the ocean.

Suddenly Graeme had an idea. They'd drive along the coast road a little way out of town, find a place to park by the beach and . . . well,

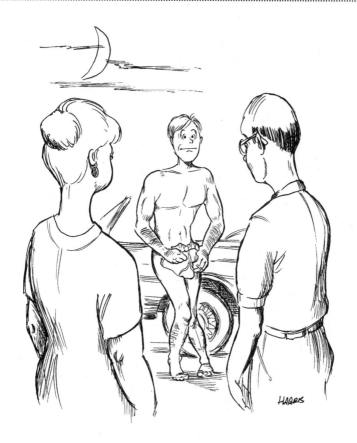

Mustang by Midnight

get romantic. A moonlit night, his lovely wife . . . and the Mustang. He just couldn't miss this opportunity.

They drove out of town in the convertible, looking for a secluded place to park. However, a lot of other people—mainly teenagers—had come up with the same idea, and every suitable spot was taken. As they drove past the parked cars, they could see the dim silhouettes of young couples locked in passionate embraces.

Eventually, they found a private location, without another car in sight. Here they were, parked in the dunes on a warm night, in complete solitude in a Mustang with the top down, and nothing between them and the twinkling stars above. As Graeme put it, "We began to imitate the teenagers we had driven past a few minutes before."

They began to pull off their clothes as their passion mounted. Just then, the headlights of another car swept across them. Graeme looked over the side of the Mustang and watched the car drive slowly past them and park some distance along the dunes. Graeme and his wife looked at each other for a moment.

"They're probably just doing what we're doing," he said.

Some fifteen minutes later, with passion spent, Graeme stepped out of the Mustang for a luxurious and satisfied stretch. Still naked, he turned to retrieve his underwear from the back seat. Suddenly, he was aware that they were not alone. The couple from the other car hadn't parked for reasons of romance. They had just wanted to take a stroll along the beach. And now they were standing about three yards away, just staring at Graeme as he writhed with embarrassment.

As he attempted to cover his not-so-private parts with his underwear held in front of him, Graeme's embarrassment quotient jumped a few notches when he recognized his surprise visitors as an elderly couple who were fellow guests at the same hotel. No doubt they recognized Graeme as well, even without his clothes on.

Wishing the ground would just open up and swallow him, Graeme finally decided he should say something.

"Er . . . good evening," he said.

The older couple looked at each other, and then back at Graeme.

"Obviously, for some," answered the man. And with that, he and his wife turned and continued on their walk.

The next morning, rather than risk facing their nocturnal visitors in the dining room, Graeme ordered their breakfast from room service, before loading their luggage in the Mustang and heading back to the car rental office.

Graeme hasn't lost his love for American cars, but he hasn't rented a Mustang in quite a while.

when bad things happen to good cops

John was a police officer in a city in Maryland. He was in his mid-twenties and single, and, unlike many of his colleagues, he couldn't wait to get back to the Police Department at the end of his shift. Perhaps there was some paperwork he could get typed up, or some files he could pull. In case you haven't guessed, there was a reason why John liked to spend his time at the station house. And the reason was Celeste.

Celeste was a secretary at the police department, and John freely admits that he was infatuated with her. She was cute and perky. She was fun to talk to. And she appeared to be interested in him too.

Naturally, John did a little detective work on the Celeste case. He discovered that she lived with her sister Lorrie, who was dating a fellow officer in the same department. Over the next week or so, John got to know the other officer a little better, and he was ecstatic when he was able to persuade Celeste to go out with him on a double date with Lorrie and her boyfriend.

In fact, they went out on several double dates, and from John's point of view, everything seemed to be progressing pretty well. They would all go out together to dinner or a movie, and Celeste gave every indication of enjoying John's company as much as he enjoyed hers.

The holidays were approaching, and they had arranged yet another double date for New Year's Eve. They would all go out to dinner, then go on to celebrate and ring in the new year. John knew that Celeste's birthday was only a few days away, and decided that this was the perfect opportunity to move their relationship up to the next level.

He went to a jewelry store in the mall and picked out a beautiful watch. He hesitated only a moment when he saw the price tag. It would take a sizable bite out of his paycheck, but it was worth it! If he was going to show Celeste how much he cared for her, it would have to be with something very special. He looked at the price tag again, and swallowed hard. Judging by the little white sticker, this would be something very special indeed. He told the clerk to gift-wrap it.

His next stop was the card shop, where he took his time selecting the card that perfectly expressed his feelings. Surely she'd love it! He would find an intimate moment after dinner to present her with the watch and the card.

His clothes. Yes, he wanted to look his best. He bought a new shirt and tie, and had his best suit cleaned and pressed. This was going to be a *great* evening!

December 31st. Dinner was planned for 7:00 P.M. John rang the doorbell and, for the umpteenth time, checked his pockets to be sure he still had the gift and the card.

Celeste's sister Lorrie opened the door, and John noticed that she didn't greet him with her customary warm smile. "Oh, er . . . hi, John," she said.

After an awkward silence, John reminded Lorrie that he'd come to get Celeste for their New Year's date. He patted the little jeweler's box in his jacket pocket.

"Look, John, there's something you should know," said Lorrie. "Celeste has met this other guy. And right now, she's upstairs in bed with him."

John stared at Lorrie. There had to be some misunderstanding. "She's in *what?*"

Lorrie looked a little uncomfortable. "Yeah, they're in bed. I don't know if you really want to wait for her. And I don't know if she'll even want to come out with us."

John knew the answers to both questions. No and no. His head was suddenly throbbing. He leaned against the wall and watched his rosy future with Celeste evaporate into thin air. He'd been so sure. . . .

Since it was New Year's Eve, the dinner had been paid for in advance, and John sure didn't have anywhere else to go. So Lorrie persuaded him to come along with her and her boyfriend and try to make the best of a bad deal.

As he was getting into his car, John turned and looked up at the faint glow showing through the curtains from the upstairs window. The watch suddenly felt very heavy in his pocket. Happy New Year, he thought. This had to be his all-time worst Date from Hell.

John now lives in North Dakota. Say, do you know anyone who wants to buy a watch?

🔱 dumb luck

Janine stepped down from the bus clutching her small suitcase, and felt the heat hit her like a body blow. But she didn't mind. Finally she was in the city of her dreams: Las Vegas, Nevada. She inhaled her first breath of hot, dry desert air. To Janine, it smelled remarkably like diesel fumes and frying onions. But not like the diesel fumes and frying onions she was used to back in her small farming town in Iowa. This was Las Vegas, and Las Vegas was special.

Janine was twenty, and for some reason she had felt irresistibly drawn to Las Vegas since she was a teenager. Movies and TV shows depicted Las Vegas as a thrilling, exciting city, teeming with sophisticated James Bond types, wearing white tuxedoes and sardonic smiles.

She had saved a little money, which she could live on for a few days, but Janine knew she needed to get a job as soon as possible. Conveniently located just across from the bus station was a small employment agency with a flashing sign in the window that read "HOTEL JOBS." Within twenty minutes, she was clutching the index card from the agency and walking into the lobby of a hotel just off the Strip. Well, quite a ways off the strip, actually. But hey, even if it wasn't the Circus Circus or The Dunes, at least this was a Las Vegas hotel and they wanted a waitess. And being a waitress was something Janine knew how to do.

The uniform of black miniskirt and frilly white blouse wasn't as revealing as those in some hotel lounges, but still Janine the farm girl felt self-conscious on her first shift. However, she quickly noted that all the other waitresses were dressed the same way, and in any case, most of the patrons were watching the show on the small stage or intent on shoving coin after coin into the slot machines that lined the walls.

She made friends with some of the other waitresses, particularly with Jilly, who was also new in town with stars in her eyes.

On her third night, one of Janine's tables was occupied by a pair of middle-aged men. Both were slightly pudgy and were puffing on large cigars. One of the men introduced himself as Bill—"They call me Hundred Dollar Bill"—and the light sparkled off his diamond cufflink as he lodged the cigar back in his mouth. His colleague said his name was Joey.

The two men stayed at the table throughout Janine's shift, and never missed an opportunity to talk to her whenever she came by. Bill hinted expansively but vaguely about various important schemes he and his partner were planning in Vegas.

"Are you guys in show business?" Janine asked eventually.

Bill's eyes flickered for a second before he replied. "Yeah, show business."

"Movies?"

"Movies, television," Bill waved a chubby hand. "Lots of things. Right?" He looked at his partner.

"Right, Bill," Joey nodded. "Lots of things."

Seeing that Janine was impressed, Bill made his move. "Listen, Baby. When you get off your shift, why don't you come up to our suite? We got a big screen TV. We're gonna watch the big fight. Closed Circuit. Whaddya say?"

Janine may have been a farm girl, but she wasn't *completely* green. Bill could tell she was dubious. He suggested she bring a friend with her. They'd order some hors d'oeuvres and champagne, watch the fight. All nice and friendly. No funny stuff. Maybe talk about Janine's show biz career. That did it. Okay, maybe she was a *little* green.

She grabbed Jilly and excitedly talked her into coming along. As they were leaving, a more worldly waitress at the hotel had a word of advice. "Watch out, kids," she said. "In this town, nothin' and nobody is quite what they seem." But Janine and Jilly weren't listening.

Bill's suite was indeed pretty spectacular. High ceilings, crystal chandeliers. Bill swept back the drapes to reveal a wide balcony with a fabulous view of Vegas spread out below. Joey was ordering shrimp platters, paté and champagne from room service. Suddenly, Janine felt a long way from Iowa. She could get used to this swanky life.

Soon, the huge TV was on, and a waiter was setting up a table of expensive goodies. Bill beckoned Janine over to the balcony, and they looked down at the millions of flashing, chasing lights and listened to the dull roar of the traffic and the milling crowds. Janine tried to look sophisticated, and managed not to cough as the smoke from Bill's cigar enveloped her head.

They heard a loud knock at the door. Bill steered Janine back inside with his arm around her waist. "Get that, will you?" he called to his partner. "That'll be the lobster tails." He turned and winked at Janine.

The moment Joey unlocked the door, it burst open, knocking him to the floor. It wasn't a waiter with lobster tails. It was a large woman in a loud floral dress and bleached blonde hair. Her cheeks were blazing red with anger, and sinews stood out on her neck like whipcords. She was trembling with barely surpressed rage as she strode into the room pointing at Bill.

"Why, you—," she advanced purposefully on Bill. "You no-good, son of a —"

Dumb Luck

Bill looked down, realized his hand was still on Janine's waist and snatched it away as if he'd touched red-hot coals. Janine could only stare at the large woman coming toward them.

"Uh . . . Roxy baby! Please!" begged Bill, wagging his flabby hands in front of him like sweaty surrender flags.

"Don't you 'Roxy baby' me!" screeched the woman. She was fumbling unsteadily in the large white patent leather purse she was carrying. "Here you are, with your mitts all over some cheap little floozie. . . ."

Janine screamed. Roxy had pulled out a large handgun and was pointing it their direction. Jilly dove into the bathroom and locked the door. Joey was moaning on the floor in a daze. And Bill definitely wasn't James Bond.

"Wait, Roxy baby," he whined, "Both these ladies are with Joey. Let me explain . . ."

Roxy wasn't in the mood for explanations. She aimed the waving muzzle in their general direction and pulled the trigger. There was an ear-splitting explosion. Janine heard glass shatter as she dove in one direction and Bill in another.

Roxy fired again. The bullet ricocheted off the ice bucket with a *peee-whing*, sending champagne, ice and green glass all over the room. Janine was terrified, convinced she was going to be killed. A vision of the headline in her Iowa newspaper flashed through her mind: LOCAL GIRL SHOT TO DEATH IN LAS VEGAS LOVE NEST. That thought was almost worse than actually getting murdered. Almost.

Bill had thrown himself behind a sofa as another bullet blew out the tube on the television. Janine pulled the table over on top of herself. The table that was full of shrimp, paté, strawberries, guacamole, salsa, and crackers, plus assorted plates, cups and glasses. One more shot rang out, and chunks of the crytal chandelier showered down on Janine.

Just then, she heard a commotion of voices and peered gingerly over the edge of the upturned table. Two burly uniformed security guards were wrestling Roxy to the floor. Quickly, Bill was at their side, assuring them that everything was okay. No, he didn't want to press charges. No need to call the police. He'd pay for all the damage. His wife had just had a few too many. Just take her somewhere to sleep it off. He stuffed several bills from a bulging money clip into the guards' breast pockets. They lifted Roxy, now half asleep in an alcoholic fog, and hauled her out the door.

Jilly emerged cautiously from the bathroom. Joey sat up rubbing his sore head. Janine crawled out from under the table. Her hair was full of broken glass. She looked down at the only good dress she owned. It was covered with mashed strawberries, salsa, and avocado slop. She felt a shrimp slither down her neck.

Bill looked at her with a weak grin. "Hey, Baby, I can get another TV sent up if you still want to watch the fight."

Janine returned to Iowa the next day, and you can bet she hasn't been back to Vegas since.

⚓ in hot water

Many of the stories collected in this book are about first dates that went horribly wrong, and ended up being last dates too. Derek's story is different. But nonetheless, it still qualifies as a Date From Hell.

Derek had been dating Janice for about a month. She was a college student, home for summer vacation, and she was a friend of one of Derek's coworkers. Derek had met Janice at a party, and after spending most of that evening together, they arranged to go out on a date.

If you've been paying attention so far, by now you're expecting to read that something terrible happened on that date. Nope. In fact, they both had a very pleasant time. They had dinner at a modest restaurant, and they thoroughly enjoyed each other's company. In fact, they went out together again on another date a few days later. By their third date, they were totally at ease in each other's company.

Derek was definitely attracted to Janice. She was bright and lively. And she was beautiful. Long blonde hair, big blue eyes, and a gorgeous figure. Being a healthy young male, Derek couldn't help fantasizing about how Janice might look . . . well, unencumbered by clothing, shall we say. But so far in their relationship, they had shared only a few kisses and cuddles, so Derek had to rely on his imagination.

But one evening, Janice suggested, "Why don't you come over to my house tonight?"

Derek had never been to Janice's house, but he knew that she lived with her parents for the summer. He wanted to see Janice, of course, but he didn't particularly look forward to sitting on the sofa watching television and being scrutinized by her mom and dad. He knew from previous experience that evenings like that can be uncomfortable, because, to most parents, no man on earth is good enough for their daughter. And usually, they make their feelings obvious.

Anyway, against his better judgment, Derek agreed to Janice's suggestion, and asked for directions to her house. Janice explained in detail how to get to her home.

"Oh, and don't come over before seven," she added, almost as an afterthought. "That's when my parents leave for the airport. They're going to Hawaii for two weeks."

As Derek hung up the phone, he felt a smile spread across his face. Home alone with Janice. This could turn out to be a very promising evening after all.

At seven-thirty, Janice opened the door and smiled warmly as she invited Derek in to the house. She looked particularly gorgeous tonight, thought Derek. She was wearing a short, sleeveless dress in a green floral pattern that showed off the perfect tan on her bare arms and legs. She leaned forward and gave him a quick kiss.

"Let me show you around," she said, taking Derek's hand.

He had to admit he was impressed by what he saw. The heavy, carved-oak dining table under the crystal chandelier. The large living room with original oil paintings on the walls. All quite different from his own cramped apartment.

Finally, Janice led him out to the deck. It was the most peaceful and secluded vista that Derek had ever seen. The custom-built wooden deck was screened by willow trees and trellis fencing with trailing shrubbery. Steps led down to a manicured lawn surrounded by mature trees and landscaped bushes. Total privacy. Complete silence. Well, *almost* complete silence.

Derek could hear a faint gurgling sound coming from a large, round, leatherlike cover on one side of the deck. Following his gaze, Janice continued the guided tour.

"That's our spa," she explained. "Here, I'll show you. Help me take the top off."

Together, they lifted the cover off the spa, and Derek gazed down at the sparkling, steaming water in the biggest hot tub he'd ever seen. Quickly, Janice pressed a few buttons. First, she turned on the romantic underwater lights, then, turning a dial, she adjusted the water from a lazy stream of bubbles to a full-thottled whirlpool, and back again.

Janice put her arms around Derek's neck, and looked at him with her huge blue eyes.

"Would you like to get in the spa with me?" she asked.

Would he?!

"I'll go to my room and change," she whispered. "You can change over there." She pointed to a small cabana beyond the spa as she went inside the house.

Cabana? I don't need no stinkin' cabana! thought Derek, as he eagerly began pulling off his clothes. He hopped, first on one foot, then on the other, as he pulled off his shoes and socks, and finally his underpants. It was like a dream come true for Derek. He remembered all those movies and soap operas he'd seen. Sophisticated

In Hot Water

couples cuddling intimately in bubbling hot tubs, while they sipped cocktails.

Cocktails! Of course. They needed cocktails. Derek remembered seeing a wet bar in the family room just through the french doors. He'd mix them a couple of martinis while Janice was upstairs. Surely Janice's dad wouldn't miss some ice and a couple of shots of gin. Totally naked, Derek padded back into the house.

As he finished mixing the drinks, he heard Janice calling his name.

"Derek," she called. Then louder and more urgently, "*Derek! Where are you?*"

Lightheaded with the excitement of it all, he held a brimming cocktail glass at arms length in each hand. "I'm he–e–re!!" he called out in a sing-song voice, as he danced out into the hallway, still naked, to meet his beloved.

There was Janice, wearing a very demure swimsuit with a towel draped around her shoulders. But this one time he hardly noticed *her.* His eyes were riveted on the middle aged couple standing beside her holding suitcases. They were gazing back at him with a mixture of shock and horror.

"Derek, this is my mom and dad," said Janice quietly. Then added unnecessarily, "Their flight was canceled."

Derek lowered the two martini glasses to approximately groin-level in front of him, trying not to spill gin on the carpet. He forced a smile.

"Hello," he said.

As he shuffled backwards toward the deck and his pile of discarded clothes, Derek knew that this was definitely not the start of a fine, long-term relationship with Janice's parents.

He was right. He saw Janice one last time before she returned to college. In a decidedly cool tone, she told Derek that if he'd bothered to look in the cabana, he'd have found a selection of swimsuits and towels provided for guests. *What was he thinking?* she wanted to know. But in the cold light of day, Derek decided that Janice really didn't want to know the answer to that question.

Derek lives in Delaware, and is trying to stay out of hot water.

PROM
TRAUMA

🔱 senior bomb

Many of our female readers are probably convinced that jerks were created specifically to make their particular lives miserable. But jerkdom is not a recent phenomenon, judging by the stories we received from a number of senior citizens.

Helen, for instance, clearly remembers her senior prom, although she is now in her sixties. Indeed, we should all remember our senior prom for a long time, but not for the same reason that Helen does. Because, for Helen, what should have been a very special event quickly degenerated into, you guessed it, a Date From Hell.

The gym looked breathtaking when Helen walked in with her date, Dave. In fact, you could hardly tell that it was a gym, because the spectacular decorations had transformed it into a glittering fantasy world. Helen couldn't remember ever feeling this excited.

The band started to play. Couples were beginning to dance, and Helen turned to Dave with a smile, ready to step onto the dance floor. But her smile faded when she saw that Dave was already dancing with another girl. Helen stood alone, her back against the wall, and waited for the song to finish. Dave would return, she was certain, and explain what had happened. Perhaps the other girl was a friend of his sister, and Dave had danced with her as a favor.

The song ended, but Dave stayed on the floor. This time he danced with a different girl. They couldn't *both* be friends of his sister. And so it went on all evening, with Dave dancing up a storm with a stream of different girls, while Helen was a wallflower, her cheeks flushed with misery and embarrassment. Sure, Dave danced with her once, when all the other girls were otherwise engaged. It wasn't the last dance, of course. That would have been too much to expect. After all, Helen was only his senior prom date!

When the prom ended, all the seniors left the gym for a prearranged dinner at a nearby swanky reastaurant. Helen was so miserable that she didn't feel much like going. But of course, she did anyway, and was swept along in the crowd of excited, laughing teenagers, feeling very much alone and sad.

The restaurant had prepared a separate room for their banquet.

It was off the main lobby at the bottom of a wide sweeping staircase. Helen isn't quite sure how it happened—perhaps her eyes were stinging with blinked-back tears. Maybe her mind was still back in the gym. In any case, she missed the first step and tumbled, head over heels, down the entire length of the staircase.

She suffered a few bruises but was otherwise unhurt. Except now her misery and embarrassment had increased a hundredfold. As the other seniors gathered around to help her to her feet, Helen noticed with horror that she had managed to rip her beautiful prom dress from hem to waist.

It was all she could do not to sob out loud as she took her seat with the other seniors and the noisy party began in earnest. Dave, in the true tradition of universal jerkdom, made no attempt to comfort her. He was too busy being the life of the party. Helen has no idea what she ate that night. Her only desire was to become invisible and put the whole awful evening behind her.

Finally, the party wound down, and Dave took Helen out to his car. They drove off, and in a few minutes, Dave steered the car into a dark, lonely lane. *Now,* of course, Dave decided it was time to turn his full attention on his date! He slid across the bench seat and began to fumble at Helen's dress with sweaty hands.

Unlike Helen, Dave was from a wealthy family who lived "on the hill," and he no doubt thought she should be honored to be on the receiving end of his groping and grappling. After a few minutes of fending off Dave's advances, Helen demanded that he take her home *now.* He sat back and stared at her in amazement. Helen could tell what he was thinking: *What's the matter with this girl? I do her the honor of letting her be my date at the Senior Prom, and now she doesn't want to "show her appreciation"?*

With a curse under his breath, this jerk of all jerks started the car and drove her home at about a hundred miles an hour, just to show her how unreasonable she was being.

It seemed as if the evening had lasted an eternity to Helen, but when she got home she was surprised to see that it was only 11:00. Her parents were surprised, too, to see her back so soon.

"Gosh, honey," said her mom, "We didn't expect you back this early! Are you all right?"

Helen looked at them and smiled. She knew that her parents, particularly her mother, had been almost as excited as she was about the prom. And she knew how much they had paid for the dress, and how little they could afford it. She carefully held the full skirt together so they couldn't see the rip.

"Yes, Mom," she answered, "I'm fine. I just have a bit of a headache, what with all the excitement."

Helen paused at the foot of the stairs and looked at her parents' faces, which were glowing with pride and happiness. How could she tell them she had just been on a Date From Hell? "I had a lovely time," she said. "Thanks for everything."

Helen Brenner is now retired and lives in Orange City, Florida. Maybe they'll have a "Senior Citizens Prom" and Helen can finally get to enjoy it!

𓂀 surprise!

Poor Cyndi. Her Date From Hell actually turned out to be a "Non–Date From Hell." She experienced the prom pain but didn't even get to enjoy the prom *dress.* She still remembers it as if it were yesterday.

Cyndi was a high school freshman, and she felt she was too young to go steady with a boy. Her parents no doubt agreed. However, when "Sam" asked her to be his date for the prom, Cyndi was more than ready to accept. She told her mother, who seemed almost as excited as she was. Cyndi and Mom managed to talk Dad into letting her go to her first prom.

Cyndi was in seventh heaven! She was finally going on a *real* date! With her mother's enthusiastic assistance, Cyndi set about her preparations for the big event. The dress would have to be ordered, of course; and then there was the hairdresser. . . .

Then, just one week before the prom, Cyndi and Sam were walking through the hall at school when another boy did one of those stupid things high school boys sometimes do. He reached out and grabbed one of Cyndi's feet as she passed his locker. He probably thought it was just a joke, some harmless horseplay. But Cyndi lost her balance, twisted around, and fell heavily. Later, at the hospital, it was determined that she had a broken ankle.

As you can guess, Cyndi was miserable. She looked at the clumpy plaster cast around her foot and knew that her first "big date" was not to be.

Two days later, Sam called her. He couldn't get the deposit back on the limo, and his tux was already paid for, he told her. Would she mind if he took someone else to the prom?

Of course I mind, Cyndi wanted to shout. But she tried to impress him with her stiff upper lip and generous nature and heard herself saying, "No, I don't mind. Go ahead and have fun."

The night of the prom, Sam called Cyndi again. "Look, I know you must be feeling bad, what with everything that's happened," he said. "Can you stay up kinda late tonight? See, after the prom, I want to bring you a surprise."

Surprise!

Of course, Cyndi agreed. She spent the evening in excited anticipation. What could this special surprise be?

Finally, the doorbell chimed, and Cyndi's mom showed Sam into the living room where the invalid sat with her throbbing foot propped up on a pillow. Sam stood before her, resplendent in tuxedo, cummerbund, bow tie, and gleaming black patent shoes.

He beamed at her. "Here!" he said, fishing something from his jacket pocket and giving it to Cyndi.

It was a Polaroid photo of Sam and his substitute date standing arm-in-arm beside the rented vintage Rolls Royce. The young lady's blonde hair was beautifully coiffed, her dress nothing short of gorgeous. Sam's eyes sparkled with the reflected warm glow from the marquee lights which also bounced off the gleaming paintwork of the luxury limousine. *Her* limousine.

"I wanted you to have this," said Sam.

You can probably imagine Cyndi's reaction to her special "surprise." Of course, *you* can imagine it, *we* can imagine it, but apparently Sam didn't have much imagination. Probably, Sam still can't figure out why Cyndi wasn't delighted by her special "surprise."

Cyndi lives in Tyler, Texas. To this day, her ankle hurts whenever she sees a Polaroid.

king for a night

rafael had been looking forward to his senior prom for the longest time. In the days leading up to the big night, he checked and double checked to make sure nothing could go wrong. He called the tuxedo rental store yet again, just to be sure that his tux would be ready on time. Yes, they told him, don't worry. He called the limousine company to confirm the pick-up time. He called the florist to be sure they would have the corsage he had ordered for his girlfriend JoAnne. Everything was prepared. Everything was double checked. Nothing could go wrong.

A Moment Made in Heaven . . .

Evenings of Champagne

Sometimes there is a gap between the time you meet that special someone, and the time the relationship gels. A gap . . . like forty-five years.

Summer 1935. That's when Sterling first met Netta at the Cincinnati School of Music. He was passing the practice room and was enveloped by the romantic sound of a Chopin étude. He was in love even before he pushed open the door and quietly stepped inside to sit entranced by the beauty of the music and of the aspiring concert pianist. Sterling soon discovered that the name of the beautiful musician was Netta, and he came to hear her play whenever he could.

Months passed, and Sterling had moved to Virginia. His best friend Bob asked him to make up a foursome with a girl named Nellie for an evening of music and dancing. As a newcomer, Sterling had no other plans and agreed to the blind date. On the appointed evening, Sterling called for Nellie, and found to his delight and astonishment that Nellie was actually his beloved pianist, Netta.

A wonderful evening was had by all, particularly by Sterling and Nellie. They laughed and danced and reveled in the music as the champagne flowed and flowed.

Nellie's mother was less than enthusiastic about her daughter's budding relationship with Sterling, and with one thing and another they drifted apart and lost touch.

The years passed. The Second World War came and went. While Sterling never really forgot Nellie, it wasn't until after the death of his wife in

---

Rafael had a particular reason for his excited anticipation. He had been told that he was a nominee for Prom King. Being nominated was an honor, but if he were to be fortunate enough to win. . . .

Thanks to Rafael's foresight, the big night seemed to be all he could have wished for, and more. At midnight, the names of the Prom King and Queen were announced. And yes! Rafael was named King!

The band played and the crowd cheered as balloons popped and confetti and streamers were strewn around in celebration. Flushed with excitement, Rafael turned to JoAnne. Something in her manner made him hesitate. And then she let him have it.

She told him in no uncertain terms that this was their last date, that he no longer wanted to go out with him. JoAnne used her obvious gift for timing to give Rafael his marching orders as they stood within a circle of his closest friends, some of whom gaped in shock

1979 that these two reconnected. During the winter of 1980, while at a concert, Sterling once again heard the Chopin étude that had drawn him to Nellie so long ago. As the music flowed around him, his thoughts went back across the years to 1935 and the practice room at the Cincinnati School of Music. He resolved to locate his long lost Nellie.

After a little detective work, he traced her to Williamsburg, Virginia. With his heart fluttering, he dialed her number. His nervousness turned to delight as he heard her familiar voice as she answered. They talked, and she revealed that she, too, was now widowed. It was decided that they would meet.

Sterling drove to Williamsburg where he found a radiant Nellie waiting with two requests. The first was for him to toast her with the chilled champagne that was nestled in the ice bucket. Secondly, he was to give her a kiss. It *had* been forty-five years, you know.

Sterling gladly complied, and he accomplished both tasks so well that they were married some three months later.

Champagne was their symbol. It became such a romantic part of their life that they came to celebrate their long-postponed love affair each and every evening. They would retire to bed at 9:30 P.M. only to awaken at midnight, whereupon they would pop open a bottle and have a dance in their private "ballroom."

They celebrated their true love story in this fashion until Nellie's death in early 1996.

Sterling, a retired executive, continues to reminisce about those days with fondest memories, and a glint of a tear.

while others were obviously enjoying this demonstration of ritual humiliation. It wasn't enough to dump him. JoAnne wanted to do it publicly.

Turning on her heel, JoAnne left Rafael to "enjoy" what was left of his night of glory. Once the show was over, his embarrassed buddies drifted away, mostly murmuring vague words of consolation. Rafael did, however, notice that Chuck, one of his so-called friends, seemed to be wearing a particularly satisfied smirk.

A few days later, Rafael discovered that JoAnne had been two-timing him with Chuck for some time before the night of the prom. Why did she choose that particular time and place to give Rafael the old heave-ho? Rafael has thought about that a good deal since then, but he has yet to come up with an answer. Of course, no one ever remembers who was the Prom King or Queen, but a messy scene like Rafael's goes down in history.

Rafael lives in Athens, Ohio. He now believes that being royalty isn't all it's cracked up to be.

COWORKERS:
KEEP IT AT
THE OFFICE

the switch

Jerry had a Date From Hell, and he wasn't even one of the "datees." This particular date was his officemate's date. At least it was supposed to be.

Jerry was a graphic designer in upstate New York. It was his first job after leaving college, and he was enjoying the novelty of a new location, new experiences, and new friends.

Jerry shared an office with Ken, one of the other designers employed by the firm. Jerry had always been an outgoing person who found it easy to make friends, so he was a little puzzled when Ken seemed to resist his attempts to get to know each other better.

Ken would only mumble an answer to any question that Jerry asked. What little conversation Ken did engage in was usually made without even looking up from his workstation. Several times, Jerry invited Ken to join him for lunch, or to visit a nearby bar and grill after work. Each time, Ken declined or just shook his head. After a couple of weeks, Jerry gave up, figuring that Ken just didn't want to pal around with him. Or maybe he was just a very private person who liked to keep his personal life to himself. Either way, Jerry wasn't offended, and for the most part, they worked together in silence.

And so Jerry was taken completely by surprise when Ken looked up from his desk one afternoon and cleared his throat.

"Um, Jerry, you want to go grab a cup of coffee after work this evening?"

"Sure," Jerry answered, trying not to look too dumbfounded. And so, a little after 5:00 P.M. they were sitting in a nearby coffee shop, at a table just barely big enough for two steaming cups of latté. Ken looked up from his cup, took a deep breath and started talking. In fact he said more in the next few minutes than he had for the previous two weeks.

He hadn't meant to be rude, he told Jerry. It was just that he had difficulty in social situations. He never seemed to know what to say, so he ended up saying nothing. "I'm just . . . you know, shy, I guess you'd call it." Jerry nodded and tried to reassure him that no offense had been taken, but Ken had something else to tell him.

"Look, I don't go on dates very much," Ken blurted out. "Well hardly at all, really. But . . . see, I asked this girl out. I don't know how, but I did. And she said yes!"

Jerry took his cue and said that was great. "No, it isn't!" said Ken, shaking his head. "I never know what to say, not at first anyway. I always think I'll say the wrong thing, and, well, you know me, I just clam up."

Jerry could see that Ken was distressed but wasn't sure why Ken was telling him all this. Then he found out.

"Can I ask you a favor?" said Ken, leaning forward. "You're great at conversation and all that stuff. I've arranged to meet Carol at a bar for a drink. Can you come along too?"

To Jerry, this sounded less than ideal, but Ken went on to explain his plan. He wanted Jerry to drop in at the bar "unexpectedly" and come over and join them. The three-way conversation would get the ball rolling and help Ken get over the first-date jitters. Once things got off to a good start, Ken was sure he'd be okay. Ken looked so miserable—even desperate—that Jerry agreed to help out, against his better judgement.

Exactly at the appointed time, Jerry entered the bar. He looked around casually, and did a good job at faking delighted surprise as he saw Ken sitting quietly at a table with a young lady. Ken beckoned him over and introduced him to Carol. Both Ken and Carol assured Jerry that he wasn't interrupting anything. In fact, Jerry noticed that Carol seemed almost as relieved as Ken when he pulled up a chair and ordered a drink.

Just as Ken had predicted, Jerry's presence helped the conversation to flow easily, and before long, all three were laughing and talking like old friends. Jerry realized that it was just about time for him to slip away quietly and leave Ken and Carol to the rest of their date. Ken must have figured this too, and decided he'd better take the opportunity to visit the men's room while Jerry was still there to keep Carol company.

As soon as Ken left the table, Carol put her hand on Jerry's arm and leaned toward him, her eyes sparkling. "Jerry, what do you say we leave now, before he gets back?" she whispered.

Jerry nearly choked on the beer he was sipping. "What? But you're Ken's date! I just came over to say hello!" he protested.

Carol would have none of it. She explained how she'd seen him make a beeline for their table as soon as he'd laid eyes on her. Then

The Switch

he'd sat down right next to her, telling her jokes and having a great time. She could tell he really liked her, and (she squeezed his arm) she liked him, too. Jerry felt the sweat break out on his brow as his eyes raked the crowded bar, searching for his returning coworker.

"But what about Ken?" he asked her. Carol snorted dismissively. She thought Ken wasn't too interested in her, anyway. After all, she pointed out, Ken had let Jerry do almost all the talking like he was bored or something. Jerry was getting seriously worried by now, and began burbling something that sounded like gibberish, even to him. Carol picked up her purse and stood up.

"Well, are you coming with me or not?" she asked with a seductive smile.

Jerry just stared at her and shook his head as he tried to find a way to salvage the situation. Carol's brow creased and her mouth turned down petulantly. "Well, it's your loss," she sneered, and pushed her way through the crowd to the door. Just then, Ken returned, his happy smile fading as he reached the table.

"Where's Carol?" he asked, his eyes searching the nearby groups of after-work drinkers. Jerry shrugged and said that Carol had had to leave. Ken looked devastated and then his face darkened with anger.

"What did you say to her? Did you tell her a dirty joke or something? What did you do? You must have done something!" Ken's voice was getting louder, and people nearby were beginning to take an interest.

Jerry just sat there, looking up at Ken. He opened and closed his mouth but no words came out. He couldn't tell Ken the truth, he decided. It would just be too hurtful.

"You ruined my date!" yelled Ken. "Thanks a lot, *pal*!" And with that, Ken stormed out of the bar, slamming the door behind him. Jerry looked around at the sea of faces that stared back at him, displaying emotions ranging from mild disapproval to abject loathing. This had not been a good idea.

When he got to work the next day, Jerry found that Ken had traded desks with another designer, and he had a new "roommate," who introduced himself as Dave. "Nice to meet you Dave," sighed Jerry. "Just don't ever ask me to go out on a date with you, okay?"

Jerry now lives in Rochester, New York, and he's finally got an office of his own.

ψ the morning after

a whirlwind romance. That was putting it mildly, thought Martin, as he stirred his tea and took another bite of toast. . . . Divorced from a marriage that hadn't worked out, Martin had moped around feeling pretty sorry for himself. Six days a week he would go to the retail clothing store in Chatham, England, where he was working as a salesman. Sometimes, it seemed he was just "going through the motions." It was obvious to Martin's coworkers—if not to Martin himself—that what he needed was some female company to cheer him up.

But Martin really didn't feel like "getting involved," as he told his coworkers when they tried to coax him into meeting some eligible woman.

His friends had almost given up on him, but Jill, one of the clerks in the accounting department, tried one last time. She suggested to Martin that he come to the local pub after the shop closed on Saturday evening. It was someone's birthday, and they were all going out to celebrate. Jill kept pressuring Martin until he agreed to come along. Jill grinned in secret triumph, because she had a plan.

At seven o'clock on Saturday, a group of the store employees paused for a moment outside the pub. Jill, arm in arm with her boyfriend, called out to Martin who was dragging along a few yards behind the others. "Come on, Martin! It's cold out here. We're waiting for you!" When Martin caught up with them, they pushed open the door and went in to the warmth and noise of the tavern.

Almost at once, Jill stopped dead, expertly feigning shocked delight. "Whoa! Look who's here!" she squealed. "Pam! I didn't expect to see *you* here!"

Within minutes, Jill had introduced Pam to Martin, then found some urgent reason to leave them alone together as she dragged her boyfriend and the others to the pool table. Martin had little choice but to order some drinks for Pam and himself, and to sit with her at a tiny table in the crowded pub.

As they began to chat, Martin realized that she was about his age, mid-twenties, and quite attractive. Actually, she was *very* attractive, he decided. Short blonde hair, petite figure, lively personality. He found himself telling her all about his interests, his likes and dislikes, even about his recent divorce. She was sympathetic, and nodded ruefully when he got to the bit about the divorce. She knew what he meant, she told him. She herself had been left with a small child, and hadn't even thought about dating. "Until now," was the silent message that passed between them.

They looked into each other's eyes, and he took her hand. They had so much in common. And she was very, *very* attractive. . . . Before too long, they were leaving the pub, and to Martin's delighted amazement, they were heading back to Pam's nearby townhouse.

And that is how Martin came to find himself sitting at Pam's kitchen table on Sunday morning, happily stirring his tea and munching a slice of toast. He sighed contentedly and stretched. He was dressed only in an old bathrobe that he had found hanging behind the bathroom door. He could hear Pam moving around in the living room, helping her young son, Joey, to get dressed.

The doorbell rang.

He heard Pam go to the window and open the curtains. "Oh no!" she said. "It's my husband."

Martin put down his teacup. "You mean your *ex*-husband, right?"

"Yeah," she answered as she went to the door. "Well, no, not really. We're not actually divorced. Just separated. I forgot he was coming over to take Joey out today."

Martin suddenly felt very cold for some reason, and pulled the bathrobe more tightly around his body. The doorbell rang again. Several times.

"He's not usually this early, 'cause he's training pretty hard every morning," said Pam. "He's hoping to get on the British Olympic team."

"Er . . . ballroom dancing?" asked Martin hopefully, his mouth dry despite the tea.

"No, don't be daft! Full contact karate. All right, I'm coming!" She unlocked and opened the door.

From the front of the house, Martin heard a deep, rumbling male voice say, "You took your time. Whose car is that outside?"

Before Pam could answer, the kitchen door opened, and Martin looked up at a massive figure that seemed to fill the door frame almost as well as the door had. Pam's husband was a beefily perfect specimen of well-muscled male, wearing a bulging T-shirt, sweatpants, and a scowl. He looked at Martin. "Who's this, the milkman?" His eyes narrowed. "And isn't that my robe he's wearing?"

Martin looked down at the garment wrapped around his body, which to him suddenly looked incredibly silly. Come to think of it, the bathrobe *had* looked a bit too large to be Pam's.

Martin tried to stretch his lips into what he hoped looked like a friendly grin. Pam's husband snorted derisively at him, and deciding that this pathetic little worm wasn't worth the effort, turned on his heel. "I'm taking Joey over to my mum's," said the deep voice, heading for the front door. "I'll have him back by five. And *he* had better be gone by then, okay?"

The door slammed. Pam came back into the kitchen and sat down at the table across from Martin, with a dreamy smile on her face. "I think he really loves me," she said thoughtfully. "Maybe we ought to give it another go." She looked at Martin and shrugged. "Sorry."

Martin didn't wait until five o'clock. He dressed quickly, grateful that, at least, he was leaving with all his teeth in place and with all limbs unfractured. This brief romance hadn't been so much a whirlwind, he decided. More like a hurricane, with him caught in the eye of the storm.

Martin finally did find "Miss Right" and is now happily married with two stepchildren.

ψ big brown eyes: a date with disaster

alex was a 17-year-old, raven-haired beauty with the biggest, brownest eyes Tony had ever looked into. He was mesmerized the moment he saw her. But she was a salesclerk and he was just a delivery boy. They were both students, spending their summer break working in a department store in London. After weeks of scheduling coffee breaks that coincided "accidentally on purpose" with hers, Tony began to build a friendship with this adorable creature. Alex was more than just a pretty face, though. She was smart, extremely funny, and her parents were wealthy. Inded, Alex was a great catch, and she knew it. She didn't play hard to get; she *was* hard to get.

Over the following weeks, after countless coffee breaks together, Alex and Tony became friends. And it seemed to Tony that she found him rather amusing. He was falling madly in love with her. He believed she felt the same way about him, but he didn't know for sure. What's more, they hadn't had one real date. They hadn't even met outside of store hours.

Then, one day, it happened. Alex invited Tony over for dinner on a Saturday night. He couldn't wait. Saturday came and he was so excited he had to pee about a hundred times. He combed his hair thirty times, and he brushed his teeth so many times his gums were bleeding when he left the house. Alex lived about two hours away by train, and she said she'd meet him at the station at 7:00 P.M.

Tony was so anxious, he took the earlier train and arrived at 6:15. He paced up and down, still feeling like he had to pee every few minutes. Alex arrived right at 7:00, and they hugged for the first time. He kissed her on the cheek, another first. She smiled at him, and those big brown eyes took his Listerined breath away once again. But this time, she was wearing an intoxicating perfume. And she was wearing it just for him! This was going to be great.

They started walking to her house. "My parents are looking forward to meeting you." Parents? On a first date? He expressed his surprise. "Your parents are having dinner with us?" he mumbled. Alex looked at him as if he were nuts. "Of course. It's their house, silly." Tony cursed silently. Oh well, we could always slip away after dinner, he thought. After a thirty-minute walk, they arrived at a very large house. Alex opened the the dark oak front door and gave him a reassuring wink. He smiled back. Maybe this would work out just fine.

Tony was immediately greeted by a tall, strong-jawed young man. Alex introduced them. "Tony, meet my boyfriend, Phil." The word *boyfriend* screamed through Tony's skull at 2,000,000 megawatts. His expression must have taken a turn for the worse, because Alex asked him if he was feeling all right. This was no longer a date. This was a nightmare. Tony's whole body now seemed numb. They sat down for dinner where his nightmare continued. Alex's mother was the headmistress of an all girls' school, and obviously a very strict disciplinarian by the way she barked at Alex's father who, it turned out, was quite deaf; Tony was sure that he was better off that way. Opposite Tony sat Alex, next to Phil, who, Tony noted miserably, was bigger, richer, and better looking than him, and also built like Thor, the God of Thunder.

Tony silently began plotting his early exit from this fiasco. But without Alex, he could never find his way back to the train station— what was he to do? They were still on the first course and this was already the longest night of his seventeen-year life. He wanted to be transported back home immediately. Conversation was minimal, and none of it was directed at him. For the next hour, he was simply an observer, an eavesdropper on Alex and Phil's vacation plans. Tony got the occasional smile from Alex, but he was now totally miserable.

Tony had stayed silent all evening and should have remained so. Unfortunately, for two idiotic seconds, he opened his big, fat mouth and stuck his foot in it, all the way down his throat. "What a dreadful painting," he announced, glancing up at a gloomy looking landscape hanging on the dining room wall. Tony's attempt at witty banter was met with a horrible clang of silver bouncing on china. Alex's mother glared at him like a hawk about to kill its prey. "That painting was done by my grandfather who was ninety years old and almost blind!" Tony's urge to pee had never been greater. He quickly apologized and, consumed with embarrassment, excused himself to the bathroom.

He glanced at his sorry reflection in the bathroom mirror, and rather pointlessly fluffed at his hair as if this one last pathetic tactic would be the one that would make Alex ditch Phil and declare her undying love for him. Good luck.

Tony flushed and exited the bathroom to return to this living hell. Alex intercepted him in the hallway. She tucked a small piece of paper into his hand. What was this? A little love note after a horrendous evening? Maybe the hair thing had worked after all. He glanced down at the paper and saw . . . detailed directions to the train station.

Tony Cane is also known as T. Kane Honey. Under one name, he writes advertising copy. Under the other, he is a country music singer. His lingering bladder problems probably date back to a certain evening in London, England.

excuses, excuses

So you went out on a Date From Hell, and somehow you lived to tell the tale. You swore, "Never again!" But Hell Dates never seem to get the message, do they? You just know you're going to get a call when you least expect it, and you'll pick up the phone, and there's that voice: "Hi, it's me. I had such a great time on our date. Can we go out again?"

If you're not prepared, almost anything can happen. Your brain may be screaming, "I'd rather be boiled alive in uric acid than ever be in the same room with you again," but somehow your lips don't get the message. "Sure, I'd love to," you hear yourself say. Now you've done it, and even a self-administered dope slap upside the head won't change it. It'll be déjà vu all over again.

Of course, you could just hang up. But you know he/she will just call right back. "I think there's something wrong with your phone. I keep getting disconnected."

No, what you need is our patented *Dates From Hell Excuse-O-Meter.* Learn these five responses by heart. No, wait. That's not enough. Make copies and keep one beside every phone in your house. Glue one to your phone at work. Wrap one around your cellular phone. Tuck one in your beeper. You just can't be too careful.

"I'M SORRY. I CAN'T SEE YOU AGAIN BECAUSE..."

(a) I'm in the witness protection program, and the Feds are making me move again.

(b) my cartel in Colombia has recalled me for remedial training.

(c) my [wife/husband/mother] has installed invisible fencing around the property, and I just can't take the electric shocks anymore.

(d) the doctors say it's much more contagious than they first thought.

(e) if my parole officer catches me outdoors after dark once more, it's the Big House again for me.

Clip and save!

ᛏ a fishy story

O *ne man's meat is another man's poison,* according to the old saying. Perhaps that should be: *"One woman's fish . . ."* We're thinking about Marigrace, who told us about an incident that occurred when she lived in in Richmond, Virginia. Of course, to you, this might not seem like a Date From Hell, unless you happen to share Marigrace's absolute hatred for any kind of seafood. Come to think of it, *"One woman's Date From Hell . . ."*

It all started when Marigrace accepted an invitation for a dinner date from a coworker. She didn't make a habit of dating men with whom she worked, but "Rick" had asked her out a couple of times before, and she'd always had some reason why she couldn't go out with him. This time she hesitated for a moment and then agreed. Dinner with Rick. Hey, it could be fun.

"Great!" said Rick. "We'll go somewhere nice. I'll pick you up at seven on Saturday."

And so, on Saturday evening, Marigrace found herself in the passenger seat of Rick's car, heading out along Richmond's "Miracle Mile." She asked Rick where they were going for dinner, but he only smiled and shook his head. "Let me surprise you," he said.

A few minutes later, Rick swung the car off the main drag and into the parking lot of a restaurant. The rain-slicked blacktop glowed crimson, reflecting the huge neon sign with the restaurant's logo: "RED LOBSTER."

Marigrace's heart sank. If there was one thing in all the world she hated, it was seafood. Maybe she'd had a bad experience as a child. Perhaps she'd gotten sick after eating a less-than-fresh piece of fish many years ago. Whatever it was, Marigrace knew one thing for sure. *She hated fish.* Just looking at a dead-eyed catfish surrounded by ice and plastic parsley at the supermarket made her stomach turn.

She turned to Rick, her mouth open, about to tell him the truth. But Rick was too quick for her.

"This place just opened a few weeks ago," he said. "I hear it's really good. I wanted to pick somewhere special for our date."

Of course, Marigrace should have said something right then. She should have, but she didn't. For one thing, she didn't want to hurt Rick's feelings. And for another, he was already out of the car, coming around to her side to open the door. Oh, well, maybe it won't be so bad, she thought.

But it was. The moment they went in, all Marigrace could smell was fried fish, broiled fish, and *yikes!* even raw fish. She was beginning to tremble even before the hostess seated them, and gave them each an oversized menu. Marigrace took one look at the menu and gulped, closing her eyes. It was the kind of menu that has pictures of all the dishes. Big color pictures of glistening crustaceans and other denizens of the deep.

Rick looked up and misinterpreted Marigrace's awestruck expression. "Yeah! Too much to choose from, right?" he asked. "Listen, order whatever you like. I've never been here before, but they say it's all good!"

Define good, thought Marigrace, but by then the waitress was at their table, pencil poised to take their order. Marigrace quickly scanned the menu, averting her eyes from the gross photographs with a shudder.

Rick and the waitress were looking at her expectantly. What was the least fishy thing on the menu? Shrimp, she guessed. At least they were small. Maybe she could persuade her stomach they were onion rings. Miserably, she ordered a shrimp platter.

"And for you, sir?" asked the waitress.

Rick flipped the menu over and pointed to an item on the back. "I'll have this," he said.

Marigrace sipped her iced tea and tried to concentrate on Rick's conversation, but all she could think of was fish. Her hair and her clothes were going to smell of seafood by the time she got home. If she got home.

She saw their waitress snaking her way through the tables toward them. Maybe she's coming to tell us that they're fresh out of seafood, fantasized Marigrace for a moment. Then she saw the tray balanced artfully against the waitress' shoulder, and realized the moment of truth was about to arrive.

The waitress placed the tray on a fold-out tray caddy behind Marigrace's chair. She reached over Marigrace's shoulder and placed an oval plate of curly pink items in front of her. Marigrace swallowed hard and tried to focus all her attention on the baked potato and the lettuce garnish.

"Your shrimp platter," said the waitress cheerfully, and turned to retrieve the second steaming plate.

"And for you, sir," she said, placing it before Rick, "Hamburger and french fries."

Marigrace stared at Rick's plate in disbelief. *Hamburger and french fries?!*

"Where . . . where did you . . . ?"

"Hmm?" said Rick, as he reached for the mustard and ketchup. "Oh, the burger? They hide this stuff on the back of the menu for people like me. I can't stand seafood! But you go ahead. Enjoy your shrimp. They look really big and juicy. . . ."

Marigrace now lives in Wisconsin, which is quite a long way from the sea. She is sure there is a very good reason that the French for "fish" is poisson. *Coincidence? You be the judge.* "One woman's poisson. . . ."

BAD TRIPS

⚡ misery in milwaukee

ometimes, you just know that a relationship isn't going to work. Nothing you can really point to, just a feeling. Then something happens that makes your brain scream, "That's it, you idiot! You're outta here!"

For Angela, that "something" was a three-day Date From Hell that must have seemed more like three months. Angela and "Chuck" lived in Nashville, Tennessee, and had been dating for several months, and Christmas was on the way. Angela's folks lived in Nashville, and Chuck's folks were in Milwaukee. Both Angela and Chuck wanted to be with their families for the holidays. As a compromise, Angela agreed to fly up with Chuck three days before Christmas and come home Christmas Eve.

Angela's first inkling of trouble came when Chuck asked her to split the cost of the plane tickets. Ever the diplomat, he also admitted that he was struggling with what to buy her for Christmas because he had run out of money. Not surprising, really: Mr. Generosity had just bought himself a couple of new motorcycles to add to his existing fleet of four or five.

They got to Milwaukee and Angela helped Chuck wrap all of his free or cheaply acquired gifts for his family. (Chuck worked for the manufacturer of the gifts, naturally.) On the twenty-third, they set off for a small town, halfway to Green Bay, because they were going to the Packers game on Christmas Eve Day. They'd be staying with an old friend of his, explained Chuck, so they wouldn't have to waste money on hotel rooms. The friend, Angela tells us, was just like Archie Bunker, except—unlike the real Mr. Bunker—this Archie and his girlfriend spent the evening smoking dope.

After a miserable night sleeping on a cold and leaky water balloon of a bed, they all squeezed into Archie's wheezy '78 Chevy and trundled off toward Green Bay. Archie pointedly told them—several times, in fact—that the tickets were twenty-four dollars each. Finally, Chuck peeked in his wallet, and sheepishly told Angela that he was a little short of cash. With a sigh, Angela paid up, but pointed out that she might have difficulty getting her car out of the long-term parking lot back home in Nashville. Chuck brushed that off as a minor problem.

Heading into Green Bay, Archie started waxing enthusiastic about a fantastic used record store he knew. As Angela gaped in astonishment, Chuck pulled out his wallet again and flipped a twenty into the front seat so Archie could buy him a few used LPs the next time he was there.

By now, Angela was livid and really ready to go home, but what could she say or do? No money for the Packers tickets, but plenty for the used LPs. The final straw came when Archie and his girlfriend lit up joints and proceeded to smoke dope in the car. Apart from almost passing out from the clouds of smoke, Angela spent the rest of the day certain that a state trooper would stop the old lurching Chevy and she'd spend Christmas in a Wisconsin jail cell.

Never was a sight so welcome to Angela as the glowing light of the Milwaukee Airport as she finally started her trip home. Later that night, back safe in Nashville, Angela closed the front door behind her and leaned against it with a sigh.

She heard the radio softly playing "I'll Be Home For Christmas" and thought, with a wry smile. "But for a while there, I sure thought I wouldn't be."

Angela is now an executive in the banking industry, and is not particularly fond of the Green Bay Packers.

ψ driving miss shelly

Shelly enjoyed going for a drive. She didn't enjoy driving herself, mind you. She liked to leave the driving to someone else, while she sat back and relaxed, happily taking in all the sights along the way.

Sadly, Shelly's love of the passenger seat resulted in a date that nearly cured her of that seemingly harmless hobby once and for all.

Shelly had met Davey through a friend of a friend, and they'd dated a couple of times. Davey seemed like a nice guy, and apparently, he loved to drive. Often his end of the conversation turned to stories about driving and the various interesting places around the country that he had visited.

One evening was going particularly well when Davey looked at his watch and sighed. "Shel, I hate to do this, but I'm going to have to call it a night. I'm driving to San Francisco tomorrow, and I want to make an early start."

Shelly's eyes lit up. "Wow. I love San Francisco. It's one of my favorite cities," she said, with visions of cable cars and quaint little harborside restaurants dancing before her.

Davey had an idea. Why didn't Shelly come along for the ride? If they left early they could grab a bite in Frisco and be back late the same day.

Shelly hesitated only a moment. She hardly ever took a sick day, and there wasn't anything pressing at work. She deserved some fun. And so it was agreed. Davey would pick up Shelly at her apartment at 5:30 A.M. the next day.

Sure enough, her doorbell rang just as dawn was breaking. There was Davey, but where was his car? Davey looked puzzled.

"Car?" He jerked his thumb proudly over his shoulder. "That's my rig, right there. Isn't she a beaut?"

Shelly squinted into the early morning haze and saw a massive black Peterbilt tractor chugging wheezily at the curb.

That? They were going to San Francisco in *that*? Davey confirmed that they were, as he helped her up into the cab. Just as soon as they hitched up the trailer at the depot.

Within minutes, Shelly was sitting in the parked tractor as Davey happily connected the trailer. Gradually, Shelly became aware of a

Driving Miss Shelly

strange and nauseating odor creeping into the cab. It became over-poweringly stronger as Davey opened the driver's side door and pulled himself up and in, whistling happily.

"What," demanded Shelly, "is that terrible stench?"

"Stench?" echoed Davey, inhaling deeply and looking about him enquiringly. "Oh, you probably mean the hogs. We're hauling hogs to San Francisco today. Didn't I tell you?"

"No," she told him, breathing through her mouth, "you didn't mention that little detail."

Davey shrugged as he set the giant rig in motion with a hiss of air brakes. He explained that he had lost his sense of smell as the result of a childhood nasal infection, so he didn't notice it. Still, he reassured his gasping passenger, they should be there in about seven hours.

"Yep, we'll pick up some burgers at the truck stop, drop these porkers off around one o'clock, and then head on back," said Davey.

"We won't be hauling hogs on the return trip, will we?" Shelly asked with much trepidation.

"Of course not," he reassured her. He consulted his clipboard with one eye still on the road. Here it was. Return load was fertilizer. All natural fertilizer.

"Oh, one other thing," said Davey. "Gets kind of hot in the cab when the sun's up, and the air conditioning doesn't work, so we'd better roll down the windows. Whoa! that smell's really getting to you isn't it?"

Shelly was curled up in the fetal position on the passenger seat, with a handkerchief pressed to her face. The California landscape passed by unnoticed.

Long before that seemingly endless day was finally over, Shelly decided that this was probably not a relationship with a future.

Shelly Welton lives in Nevada. She hasn't visited San Francisco—or eaten bacon—in quite some time.

⚡ queen of possum kingdom

nnamarie was sitting in the passenger seat as her date, Howard, drove. This was their first date, and they were heading out of Dallas on the way to Possum Kingdom, a little Texas hamlet where Howard and his band had a gig scheduled for that evening.

Annamarie couldn't help her frequent glances at Howard's "hair." Her friend Glenda—who had set up this date with Howard, a friend of her own boyfriend—had forewarned her that Howard was almost completely bald. However, in the meantime Howard had apparently visited a bargain-basement Hair Club knockoff, and he looked as if a particularly scruffy stray kitten had taken up residence on his scalp.

It was pretty obvious that Howard had fortified himself with a few drinks before setting off. And what does someone do when they have a two-hour drive and a new date to impress? Buy more liquor, of course. As soon as they got out of the "dry" county and into "wet" territory, Annamarie could almost see Howard salivate in anticipation.

Howard pulled off the road at a convenience store in a not-so-lovely neighborhood, and left Annamarie in the car while he went in to stock up on fresh "supplies." She looked out of the window and decided she was safer inside the car rather than outside, even allowing for Howard's blood-alcohol level.

Before long, they were on the road again. For about an hour or so, Howard regaled her with his complete repertoire of "humorous" stories and impressions. He seemed to believe he was a comedian as well as a musician.

"Okay, here's Dana Carvey doing an impression of George Bush doing an impression of Mick Jagger! Whaddya think?" asked Howard. Annamarie thought that Howard should concentrate a little more on his driving.

As they approached Possum Kingdom, Howard chattered on about the nightclub they had contracted to play in. His excitement dwindled when they pulled up in front of the venue. It was a dilapidated windowless cinder-block building with a half-moon cut in the front door. With a sinking feeling, they walked in.

The club owners were behind the bar. They introduced themselves as Stuart and Betty, and Betty immediately told Annamarie that she had just had breast enhancement surgery. She proudly pointed at her new accessories, which were struggling to escape from her '70s-style halter top. She offered Annamarie a drink. A vodka tonic? Well, there was vodka, but no tonic. No call for it. Betty handed her a paper cup, explaining that she was saving the *real* ones for the customers. "Expecting a rush, what with the band an' all."

The other band members arrived, eyeing their venue like victims of shellshock. Howard had somehow managed to control his initial disillusionment, and he was now happily slugging down beer after beer as the place began to fill up.

When Howard and his band took the stage, a one-eyed Mexican cowboy slid onto the bar stool beside Annamarie. He introduced himself as Juan and immediately began a continuous attempt to get her go out to the parking lot with him. Desperate for any kind of conversation that involved less saliva and more verbs, Annamarie concentrated on talking to Betty, whose main topic of conversation was her new and expensive pair of breasts.

The band took a break, and Howard ordered another drink, despite Annamarie's pleas to take it easy, considering the long drive home. She walked him to the parking lot for a breath of fresh air.

The cool night air combined with the alcohol had an odd effect on Howard. He leaned against his car and began to cry long heartbreaking sobs. He was pining for his estranged wife who refused to speak to him anymore. Annamarie shook her head and wondered what she had ever done to deserve this. Gradually she calmed him down. As his sobs turned to sniffles, Howard took her face tenderly in his hands and proclaimed undying love for her. Annamarie rolled her eyes heavenwards. Oh, puh-leeeze! She led him back inside to begin the second set and took her seat next to Juan at the bar.

She noticed that Stuart was motioning for her to come over to the end of the bar and join him and Betty. They both looked quite solemn, and Annamarie guessed they were about to complain about the band, which sounded awful to her ears, and she imagined it must be pretty bad even by Possum Kingdom's standards. Not so.

Stuart cleared his throat. "Annamarie, Betty and I have talked it over and we won't take no for an answer. We want you and your fiancé to come live here in Possum Kingdom an' run our country store!"

Fiancé?!

Okay, Annamarie told herself. That's it. Time to go *now*. She'd had enough of this club, enough of Juan, enough of Possum Kingdom, and enough of Howard. And just how many people had he told that they were engaged?

As soon as the set ended, she dragged Howard out to the car, smiling and promising Stuart and Betty that she and Howard would absolutely return the following weekend for the annual Possum barbecue festival. *Right.*

They got in the car and Howard straightened his hair and began to relive their exciting adventure. Annamarie turned her steely eyes on him.

"Shut up! Just shut up and drive me home. Don't say another word. And if you ever see me at the grocery store or at a baseball game, or *anywhere,* just keep on walking!"

Howard did as he was told.

Annamarie still lives in Texas but has never sampled possum barbecue.

A Moment Made in Heaven . . .

Under the Golden Gate Bridge

Gentlemen, you could learn a lot from Dean when it comes to creating a romantic moment. . . . Joanie and Dean had both had their share of "nightmare encounters of the dating kind" before they finally found each other.

Joanie tells us that, right from the start, Dean was very creative when it came to dating. She never knew quite what to expect.

For instance, early in their relationship, Dean arrived at her house driving a large van instead of his usual car. When Joanie climbed into the van, she found all the comforts of home. Literally. You see, Dean had outfitted the van with furniture from the living room in his apartment. It was all there. Carpet, sofa, arm chairs, pictures on the wall, drinks, and soft music. If Joanie wouldn't come to his apartment, his apartment would come to Joanie.

But now let us move ahead to a true "moment made in heaven."

After two years of dating, Dean and Joanie had never discussed marriage. Yes, Joanie says, she had thought about the possibility, but it just hadn't been something they had talked about.

Dean is a photographer, and he never misses an opportunity to add to his supply of "stock" photos. Their trip to San Francisco wasn't any different, except that, on this occasion, Joanie was suffering from a cold that was threatening to evolve into flu. Dean had planned to visit the marina to take some more stock shots, and he wanted Joanie to come with him. Joanie had other ideas. She'd just stay in the hotel room and nurse her cold. But Dean was persistent, and finally she gave in and agreed to go along.

As they got out of the cab at the marina, a man wearing a captain's cap stepped forward. "Mr. Dixon," he said, "Your yacht awaits."

The captain saluted smartly and, turning on his heel, led the way along the dock. An amazed Joanie just couldn't imagine what was going on, but knowing Dean and his creative way with surprise dates, she knew it was likely to be a delight.

Joanie was right. The captain and his first mate helped them aboard a beautiful vintage yacht that dated from a time when burnished walnut and gleaming brass were the standard maritime accoutrements. As the majestic craft nosed out of the marina, Joanie forgot her cold and marveled again at Dean's romantic streak. But there was more to come.

At sunset, they passed under San Francisco's famous trademark, the Golden Gate Bridge. The bridge was living up to its name, reflecting the last golden rays of the setting sun. At that moment, Dean pulled a little black box from his pants pocket. He opened it slowly and something sparkled from its dark velvet center.

"Wanna get married?"

Joanie stood there in shock. No words would come. Again, he asked her, "Wanna get married?"

Finally, she managed to nod as her mouth opened and closed silently, and the tears began to flow. Moments later, the captain appeared on deck. Had she accepted? he asked Dean. When Dean confirmed that she had, the captain nodded to the first mate, who stepped forward with a bottle of champagne and a dozen long-stemmed roses.

Joanie accepted the captain's invitation to make a ship-to-shore phone call to tell her mother the news, then settled back to enjoy the rest of the private cruise with her new fiancé. The remaining days in San Francisco are now a blur in Joanie's memory, as the sparkle from her diamond ring blinded her to anything else. But she knows that she will never forget that magical moment under the Golden Gate Bridge.

Dean Dixon is the kind of guy who could teach a class on creating the perfect date.

⚡ i'm dreaming of a french christmas

"**I** wanna go home!" Terry stared at the woman who had wailed those words. His mouth hung open in amazement as he struggled to reply. It was Christmas Eve. They were standing at the front door of his vacation cottage nestled in the picturesque southwest of France. They had just driven five hundred and fifty miles from the French coastal town of Calais after taking the ferry from Dover, England. He was tired and his back ached, and he was looking forward to the bottle of champagne that he knew his neighbor had put in the refrigerator as a Christmas gift.

And his date stood on the doorstep, lower lip trembling, and said it again: "I wanna go home!"

Terry had seen Toni's personal ad in his local newspaper, and he replied, including a photo of himself standing on the veranda of his French cottage. They had arranged to meet initially in a local hotel lounge, and, says Terry, they really hit it off. They were about the same age; both were approaching what is politely called "middle age." Terry noted her trim figure, pretty face framed by blonde hair, and her lively personality.

They met a few more times, and Terry suggested that for a very special date Toni should spend Christmas week with him at his cottage in France. He'd be happy to drive her there in his car, and he would make reservations at a wonderful restaurant in the village. Toni thought this sounded wonderful, but with one condition: They should have separate bedrooms. Ever the English gentleman, Terry readily agreed.

The day began perfectly. As they waited for ferry at Dover, they walked together along the wharf, looking up at the wheeling seagulls squawking above them in the pale blue winter sky.

Before long, they were speeding south through the French countryside. The weather was deteriorating, and a snowstorm around Orleans slowed them down as Terry peered through the swishing wipers into the grey swirl ahead. To make matters worse, Terry noticed that the car seemed to be handling badly. He nursed the car to a small garage just outside Bergerac, where a morose mechanic confirmed with a Gallic shrug that *monsieur* had a slow flat, and would need a new tire. A very expensive one, of course. *Merci.*

By now, Toni was beginning to sneeze and complain about a pain in her chest. Terry tried without success to find a pharmacy open on Christmas Eve as they drove through the scattered French villages. Anyway, it didn't seem to be much more than a mild cold.

Eventually, Terry pulled the car onto the gravel in front of his cottage and got out stiffly, rubbing his aching back. Toni climbed out too, and looked, sniffling, at the cottage.

"I wanna go home!"

With a sigh, Terry unlocked the door and ushered her inside, noting that his neighbor had turned on the heat and aired the bedsheets and blankets, in addition to putting a bottle of bubbly on ice.

Toni began to complain that the house was small, it was cold, and she felt sick. She wanted to see a doctor. Now. Amazingly, Terry managed to locate a doctor who was willing to come out to the cottage. For a price, of course. Terry took the doctor's prescription to a pharmacy, and headed back gloomily to the cottage. Unfortunately, Toni was, if anything, even more unhappy by then.

Terry watched in dismay as a middle-aged woman reverted to a petulant five-year-old before his eyes. She kept telling him that she didn't like it here. She demanded a bowl of soup, then refused to eat it. She said she didn't want to be around Terry, then insisted that he not leave her alone when he suggested he go out and get something to eat. As midnight approached, Toni found a telephone book, and called the local airport. Not surprisingly, there were no flights leaving for England on Christmas Day, so Toni booked herself on a flight early on the morning of the twenty-sixth.

Terry's vision of a romantic Christmas Day dinner at one of France's better restaurants was rapidly fading. He realized that he was destined to spend the next thirty hours or so with someone who now seemed to be, well, *emotionally unstable*, to put it nicely.

Throughout that night, Terry was awakened by a peevish Toni knocking on his bedroom door demanding affection only to push him away within minutes and head to the bathroom to run herself yet another hot bath. After each bath, just as Terry was dropping off to sleep, there would be another insistent tapping on his door, and the cycle would start over again.

When a wintery dawn finally broke on Christmas morning, Toni insisted on seeing the doctor again. A decidedly disagreeable physician arrived, muttering uncomplimentary things about the English in general and present company in particular. He diagnosed panic attacks, and gave Terry a supply of Valium with instructions to administer only one tablet at a time and only when the patient was suffering an attack.

Throughout Christmas Day and the night that followed, Terry was tempted to give in to Toni's ever more strident demands that he give her the entire bottle. But somehow, he managed, bleary eyed, hungry and depressed, to follow the doctor's instructions.

December 26th arrived at last, and Terry drove his still-complaining guest to the airport and bundled her, thankfully, onto the plane. Finally brightening up for the first time since he left Dover, he found himself whistling a little tune as he returned alone to his cottage. He decided he'd open the champagne after all. Now, at last, he had something to celebrate.

Terry lives in southern England. When he reads the newspaper these days, he tends to skip the personals.

DANGER
DATES

ice? what ice?

eslie's Date From Hell actually turned out to be a Date *in* Hell—Hell's Hollow, Tennessee, that is. The date started well enough. It was a crisp, cold February evening that seemed tailor-made for the hearty dinner that Leslie enjoyed at Bud's Catfish with her date, Jim.

After dinner, Jim suggested they drive out to Hale's Hollow to admire the moonlit scenery. Now, Hale's Hollow is the real name of this particular stretch of land. It had belonged to old man Hale, an unsociable loner who had holed up there most of his life. But most of the locals called it "Hell's Holler," because the words "Hale" and "Hell" can sound mighty similar when you say them with a southern accent. At least, that's *one* explanation. . . .

The climbed into Jim's pickup truck and set off. The roads were slick with patches of thin ice, and the fields on either side reflected the moonlight from their blankets of snow. Turning off the highway, Jim steered down the track into Hale's Hollow. Leslie had figured that they would pull in a few yards, take a look around, then head on home. Jim had other ideas.

Insisting that his truck was up to the task, Jim drove on down the track, bumping and sliding through the mud and snow. About a mile in, they rounded a bend between clumps of towering fir trees, and approached what appeared to be a small lake of ice. "Don't worry, Les," Jim said. "We can make it."

Well, they didn't. Jim tried rocking the truck back and forth: reverse, forward, reverse, forward. Reluctantly, Leslie climbed out of the truck into water that resembled a mud slushie from the Seven Eleven. A light snow began to fall as she leaned against the bumper and pushed. The wheels spun. The mud flew. The truck stayed stuck.

When it became apparent that the truck was not going anywhere, there was nothing else to do but head back up to the highway on foot. There was one blanket in the truck, and Leslie hoped that Jim would be gentleman Jim and let her have it. No such luck. "We fought for that blanket the entire way," recalls Leslie.

Ice? What Ice?

Freezing cold, soaked and muddy, and struggling up a rutted track in squelching shoes, Leslie decided the locals were right about this place. It *was* Hell's Holler.

Leslie Liles-Maxwell is Marketing & Development Coordinator for Progress, Inc., a non-profit organization serving people with disabilities.

⚰ death valley death wish

because dating and driving seem to be so irrevocably intertwined, it is no surprise that automobiles seem to figure in their fair share of Dates From Hell.

Just ask Karen, for instance. Her dating nightmare happened back in the summer of 1986, and, she says, she can still remember every traumatic moment of it.

Karen was on a date with "Phil," one of her brother's friends, whom she had just met. They were driving in Phil's beat up old pickup truck in the foothills of California, just north of Sacramento. Phil was nice enough and seemed to be a reasonably intelligent person. But Karen was soon to discover that her usually reliable woman's intuition was off. Way off.

When the time came for Phil to drive her the twenty or so mostly mountainous miles to her home in the valley, he suddenly boasted that he had mastered the skill of driving that particular stretch of winding, hilly, dangerous highway in twelve minutes flat! Obviously, he assumed this would impress Karen. She, on the other hand, had immediately concluded that he was a brainless idiot with a death wish.

With that, he set out to prove his masculinity by demonstrating this incredibly dumb feat. Downshifting through the transmission and with tortured tires screaming, he threw the hurtling pickup into every hairpin curve at top speed.

Needless to say, Karen was completely hysterical throughout the entire ordeal, crying and begging him to stop and let her out. Deaf to her pleas, Phil continued to pass other vehicles on hills and blind curves, often with all four wheels off the ground at the same time.

Somehow, they made it to Karen's house unscathed, and trembling with a mixture of fear, shock, and relief she told Phil that under no circumstances would she ever speak to him again.

Amazingly, two years later, Phil showed up on Karen's front porch. He had two questions for her. First, why had she changed her telephone number? And second, would she like to go out with him again?

Karen stared at him for a moment in stunned silence. She shook her head, and quietly closed the door.

Karen May continues to live in California. For some reason, she doesn't like riding in pickup trucks.

⚡ delayed reaction

Most of the time, though you may not admit it, you can tell right away that you're not only on a Date From Hell, but you're on a runaway bus that is careening off the cliff into the jaws of Dating Hades. You just know that this thing is doomed from the start.

But sometimes, you don't see it. Not at the time, anyway.

Take Jodi, for instance. Jodi lives in Texas. Some time ago, she dated a man we'll call Art. They'd met somewhere, and he seemed nice. Art asked her out, and Jodi accepted.

So they went out together, and for a while, Jodi was kind of hoping that it would develop into a more serious relationship. But it didn't. And for one very good reason. One day Jodi got a call from Art's wife. Somehow, Art had neglected to mention that he was married and the father of a baby boy. Just slipped his mind, probably. Not surprisingly, Jodi broke it off with Art, and eventually she pretty much forgot about him.

Until she picked up a newspaper one day and began reading a story about the disappearance and presumed murder of a woman. The prime suspect was the woman's boyfriend. And then a name jumped off the page at Jodi. Was it a coincidence? No, there was his age too. Everything matched. And there was a photo of the suspect. He'd changed since she'd seen him, but there was no mistake. The man that police believed had murdered his girlfriend was none other than Jodi's former date. It was Art.

"A goose walked over my grave when I read it," said Jodi.

That poor woman could have been me, she thought. As she put down the newspaper, she cast her mind back to that date with Art, all that time ago.

Twenty five years ago, to be exact.

Yes, it took a quarter of a century for Jodi to realize how close she had come to having a *real* Date From Hell.

Jodi is an English instructor, and still lives in Texas. She firmly believes that, sometimes, God's greatest gifts are unanswered prayers.

men: top ten ways to ensure you have a date from hell

10. Don't ask where she'd like to go. What does she know, anyway?

9. Rely on your faultless inspiration. You'll come up with something neat at the last minute. Probably.

8. Take your two rottweillers in your car to the vet to see about their constant diarrhea and vomiting. Do this just before you pick up your date. Hey, she said she liked animals, didn't she?

7. Don't bother to shower before you meet your date. Especially after a rigorous hour or so of hoops with your buddies. So what if you're steaming like a racehorse? You're a manly kind of guy and she ought to appreciate that.

6. Be sure to put on your evilest-smelling shoes and the cut-offs you wear to change the oil in your pickup. The Hooters T-shirt would be a nice touch too.

5. Be sure she notices those charming bumper stickers on the back of your car. Especially the one that says: "NO FAT CHICKS."

4. Tell her about all the babes you've dated. *All* of them, now. Describe their awesome breasts and their remarkable sexual agility. Go into detail.

3. At the restaurant, do that thing you do with the straws up your nose. It really is funny.

2. Don't forget your Groucho Marx impressions. Stay in character for the entire evening. Follow the waiters around in a Groucho slouch while you pretend to smoke a cigar. Sidesplitting.

And of course . . .

1. Have several drinks before for your date. It makes you much more interesting. And try to continue drinking throughout the evening. Just to "keep that buzz."

☥ hot fruit

Why is it that a lot of guys feel they have to pull some dopey stunt in order to impress their dates? Is it that the giddy excitement of being with someone new overwhelms their normal common sense? Or is it that they act like morons all the time, and the unfortunate women who date them get to sample just one awful evening from a lifetime of awfulness? Or could it be that 99.99% of men are caring, sensitive, thoughtful creatures, and we're just hearing about the errant 0.01% in these stories? Could that be it?

Nah.

Take the story we heard from Mary, for instance.

She went out on a date with a man we'll call Bill. The date went okay. Nothing special but nothing that was a real turn-off, either. Nothing, that is, until he was driving her home after they left the restaurant.

They were talking about food in the car, and discussing what they liked and didn't like, as they drove the forty-five miles or so along the state highway that passed through rolling meadows and farmland.

"Do you like watermelon?" asked Bill.

Mary innocently agreed that, yes, she did enjoy a nice fresh watermelon.

With that, Bill wrenched the wheel over and sent the car off the road and bumping into a field. A shocked and speechless Mary watched Bill leap from the car and scurry off into the pitch black night. All she could hear was Bill grunting and some strange rustling sounds. Within a few minutes, he was back.

He opened the car door and pushed two huge watermelons across the seat at Mary.

"Oh, my God!" wailed Mary, whose stomach was knotted in terror. "You've stolen them! You idiot—we're gonna get shot!"

She peered frantically into the inky darkness on both sides of the car, convinced that shotgun-waving farmers were about to descend upon them. Bill's brow wrinkled as he looked at Mary. He had no idea what was wrong.

"But you said you like watermelon!" said Bill with a shrug.

Hot Fruit

"Look, forget it! Forget it! Let's just get out of here," hissed Mary, craning her neck toward the road, searching the gloom for blue flashing lights.

Heaving a sigh, Bill climbed into the car and shook his head. As the car bumped back onto the highway, Mary heard him mutter under his breath, "Women!"

No doubt Bill was puzzled when Mary declined his invitation for a second date.

Mary doesn't want to say where she lives. Just in case an agricultural hit squad still has a contract out on her.

141

THE SECOND
IMPRESSION'S
THE KILLER

⚡ truly clueless

One of the best movie titles in the past few years was *Clueless*. Now that's a title (and a description) that could be applied to many of the men who "star" in these dating stories. Yes, we're sorry guys, but, unlike the movie, the "clueless" tag seems to apply almost exclusively to men when it comes to not having a clue about dating etiquette.

Case in point: Jim. Eileen was introduced to Jim, a friend-of-a-friend. They met for the first time at a bar on the Jersey Shore. Eileen thought he was cute and well dressed, and he seemed to be a nice guy. She agreed to go on a date with him.

They decided to go out together the following Saturday afternoon. Like any woman would, Eileen went to the mall and bought a new outfit that would be ideal for a pleasant, casual late afternoon/early evening date.

Saturday. As Eileen was putting the finishing touches to her makeup, she heard the doorbell ring, and then the sound of her roommate answering it and letting Jim into their apartment. Within a few moments, her roommate came into Eileen's bathroom and quietly closed the door. She looked at Eileen's clothes.

"You might want to change into something more casual," she advised.

Eileen looked down at what she was wearing. "Don't be ridiculous! This is casual!"

The roommate shook her head. "Not casual *enough*."

Emerging from the bathroom, Eileen saw her date. He was dressed in a dirty sleeveless T-shirt and cut-off blue jeans with holes in them. Holes big enough to reveal the red boxer shorts he was wearing. Rolled-down white (well, white*ish*) socks and a pair of ratty sneakers completed Jim's dating couture.

At this point, Eileen wanted to do a quick U-turn back into the bathroom, but decided to give him a chance. Maybe he hadn't had time to change after work and would stop off at home on the way. Sadly, it was not to be.

For some reason that never became clear, Jim took her to a friend's house. A married friend with two very overactive kids and a large sheepdog. (By the way, Eileen is allergic to dogs; and she's not real crazy about overactive kids either.) Jim then disappeared for forty-five minutes, leaving Eileen alone with this bunch of total strangers. And just to raise the tension level a few notches, there were two pet birds loose in the room, who took turns seeing how close they could swoosh past Eileen's face.

When Jim returned—giving no clue as to where he had been—he asked Eileen if she was hungry and felt like some dinner. Anything, even a burger joint, would be better than staying where she was, so she readily agreed, and they headed out to Jim's car.

Truly Clueless

Before long, Jim pulled up outside a Chinese restaurant. With the engine still running he turned to Eileen. "Whaddya want to eat?" he asked.

"Well, I guess I'll wait 'til I get inside," she answered, opening the passenger door.

"Nah," said Jim, waving her back into her seat, "I'll just run in and get some take-out."

Eileen curtly told him that she wasn't hungry anymore. Our clueless hero shrugged and shambled into the restaurant. A few minutes later, he reappeared, carrying a steaming, smelly paper sack, which he plunked on the bench seat between them.

Jim then insisted on showing Eileen his "log cabin." Beginning to feel like a prisoner, and looking forward to the end of the evening, Eileen had little choice but to go with her dopey date to his rustic hideaway.

When they arrived at Jim's cabin—little more than a shack, really—Eileen looked around miserably. "Er . . . where's the bathroom?" she asked.

Jim shrugged. "No indoor plumbing out here. Sorry." He waved in the general direction of the door, presumably indicating the conveniently located trees and bushes to be found outside.

Apparently oblivious to Eileen's anger, discomfort, and misery, Jim flopped down and attempted to eat his wonton soup with chopsticks. Very noisily. When he was finally through with his dinner, he apparently decided it was time to get romantic. Eileen had other ideas, and after several requests he agreed to drive her home.

Needless to say, this was their first and last date. But really, look at it from Jim's point of view: He'd dressed nice. Kinda casual, but, it was Saturday, wasn't it? And they'd had some nice social time with his friends. Then he'd offered to buy her something to eat. Not his fault if she wasn't hungry, right? And he'd taken her to his secluded, romantic hideaway for a night of romance, and she didn't like that either. Women! Go figure! Like we said: Truly clueless.

Eileen lives in New Jersey, and when friends tell her they know "a really cute guy," she says, "Thanks, but no thanks!"

☿ you thought i was what?

algernon was feeling pretty good, and with good reason. He seemed to be hitting it off really well with Cheryl. They were attending the same college and had met on campus. Algernon found out that he and Cheryl had a lot in common. They were both majoring in political science, and they shared the same sense of humor. They talked and laughed together several late nights in a row.

After having coffee together a few times, Algernon asked Cheryl to dinner, and he was delighted when she quickly accepted.

Algernon made a reservation at his favorite upscale restaurant. It was a little pricey, but he figured it was worth it for a dinner date with Cheryl. The meal was wonderful, the lights were suitably dim, and in this ideal romantic ambience, Algernon felt the evening was going perfectly. Until . . .

Until Algernon said something. He says that, to this day, he can't remember exactly what it was. But in any case, he said *something,* and Cheryl froze, eyes wide and fork halfway between plate and mouth.

There was a sudden deafening silence, until Cheryl again found her voice.

"But—but I thought you were gay!"

Algernon stared at his date. Perhaps he had misheard her. Quietly, he asked her, "You, er, thought I was what?"

He hadn't misheard. Cheryl had been convinced that Algernon was gay, and that was why she had accepted his dinner invitation.

Algernon was mortified. Cheryl blurted out that she had confided in him, spent all this time with him, precisely because she thought he was gay. She had told him things thinking he was "safe," she said.

And all along, Algernon had interpreted all this as "hitting it off great." The rest of the meal tasted like dust in his mouth as he tried to hide his disappointment from Cheryl, who, in fairness, must have been feeling pretty embarrassed herself.

Understandly, Algernon and Cheryl did not date again. They remained friends, and he's always pleased to see her when they meet. But, Algernon says, he still gets "a bit squirmy inside" whenever he sees her.

Algernon says that he learned an important lesson from this experience: Never take a first date to an expensive reastaurant!

Algernon Whitefield lives in Louisville, Kentucky. And he's not gay. Not that there's anything wrong with that.

A Moment Made in Heaven . . .

Petals

Michael had the charm and charisma of a European. Susan was a local girl, attractive in her own way, and mesmerized by her dashing prince.

Their relationship grew and blossomed, but then Susan began to notice that Michael was sometimes distracted. At first she tried to ignore it, but more and more, it became apparent that something was bothering him. Susan worried that perhaps she was the cause of his increasing distress. Eventually, she confronted him with her concerns.

He assured Susan that it was nothing she had done. He was facing potential ruin as his previously firm financial footing began to crumble beneath him. Apart from anything else, Michael confessed, he was afraid he would lose her, too, as his financial status changed.

Like a true country girl, Susan *stood by her man.* She encouraged him. She reminded him of his many talents. She gave him back his confidence. And most of all, she assured him that she would be there for him.

One evening, a few days later, a newly confident Michael relayed to Susan his sincere appreciation for her support, and told her how special she was to him. This has been tough on you, too, he told her. You need to relax, he added. Michael persuaded Susan to pamper herself with a long, luxurious and well-deserved bubble bath.

After an indulgent half-hour in the steamy bathtub, Susan returned to the bedroom, and found the loveliest and most romantic surprise of her life. Soft music was playing. A bottle of Kristal champagne was chilling in a silver bucket of crushed ice. And the bed linens were completely covered in fresh, fragrant, red rose petals. . . .

Clearly, the prince, while he may have been losing his financial empire, never lost his charm.

Susan J., an executive, has significantly expanded her garden with various types of roses.

☙ ooh! that voice!

greg is a successful photographer who lives in the South. His work can be seen on calendars, billboards, advertisements, and CD covers all across America. He remembers the early days, when he first opened his own photography studio and was a younger and, perhaps, less worldly guy.

To ensure that he did not miss any calls from potential clients, Greg hired a telephone answering service. Several times a day, Greg called in for his messages. Perhaps, if truth be told, he called in more often than was really necessary, because the woman assigned to his line had the most sultry, enticing voice he had ever heard. Sometimes, just listening to her speak, Greg forgot why he had called in the first place.

She must have felt the same way, because she suggested they meet sometime. In fact, she continued to suggest it, to the point of insisting. Against his better judgment, but dying of curiosity, Greg agreed to meet this sultry voice one evening, a vision of loveliness dancing in his imagination.

Arriving at her apartment with combed hair and a big smile, he pressed the bell. Immediately, the door flew open, and Greg's jaw dropped. Before him stood a woman—he hoped!—at least twice his size wearing a lupine leer and a ten-gallon cowboy hat. Immediately, Greg was struck by her resemblance to a famous country music singer. Unfortunately, that singer was Charlie Daniels.

Greg found himself being ushered inside and propelled toward a creaky sofa. As soon as he was seated, the sultry-voiced siren purred, "Honey, I've waited six months to do this!" Drawing him to her with powerful arms, she puckered up and gave him a great big sloppy kiss.

Within minutes, her conversation turned to the subject of bisexuality. Enough was more than enough by this time, and babbling incoherently, Greg flew out the door, beet red from embarrassment.

After that incident, Greg determined to keep his fantasies firmly locked up in his imagination.

These days, Greg has an answering machine.

Ooh! That Voice!

⚛ top tan tenor

What could be more romantic than having your date serenade you? Well, having a tooth pulled might come to mind, if you happen to be Stacee, that is.

Stacee had recently moved to Portland from Seattle, and was just beginning to find her way around her new city. Seeing her reflection in the bathroom mirror one morning, she decided that she was looking a little pale and pasty. Not at all the way an unattached young lady in a new city should appear. Especially if she expected to make an impression on Portland's unattached young men.

A tanning salon. That was the answer. She had noticed one close to where she worked, and decided to stop by that evening and sign up.

When Stacee pushed open the door to the tanning salon, she was immediately impressed. Not by the modern decor, nor by the clean and tidy layout. Not even by the state-of-the-art tanning equipment. Nope. What caught her eye was the handsome young man behind the reception desk.

Tall. Blond. Gleaming white teeth emphasized (of course) by a deep golden tan. His name was Stan, according to the nametag attached to the tight polo shirt he was wearing.

Wow, thought Stacee. Things are definitely looking up.

Stacee soon became a regular patron of the tanning salon, and made sure that Stan knew she was single and available. Finally, Stan got the message and asked her out for a date.

Portland really was beginning to look good to Stacee. With two days to go before her date with golden boy Stan, she had just enough time to select the right outfit and get an appointment at the hair salon.

The afternoon of the date, Stacee was surprised to get a call from Stan. He was still at work, and he had forgotten to tell her that he had neither a car nor a driver's license. She'd have to come and pick him up at the tanning salon, he said, and take him to his apartment so he could get changed.

Stacee was beginning to hear faint alarm bells from off in the back of her mind. But being new in town and without a date, she decided to take a chance.

Before long, Stan was in the passenger seat of her car, giving her the directions to his apartment.

It took him only a minute to change his clothes and soon he had fixed them both a drink, and was sitting next to Stacee on the sofa. They talked for about half an hour about this and that. Places to go in Portland. Movies they both liked.

And then Stan started singing.

Not the intimate, quietly whispering in your ear type singing. Not the kind you might expect from someone whose mouth was three inches from your face.

No. Stan was singing loud. Really loud. Belting out a soulful Boyz 2 Men type of song. As if he was on stage at Radio City Music Hall, and Stacee's head was the microphone.

Stacee was astonished. He hadn't led up to it in any way. He hadn't even mentioned songs or singing. One minute he was talking, the next he was crooning into her face at the top of his lungs.

The song dragged on and on. And on. Cringing with embarrassment, Stacee wondered if he would ever stop. Maybe this was a nightmare, and she would wake up any minute. But it wasn't, and she didn't.

Finally Stan got to the "big finish" and sat back beaming at her. After a second, Stacee collected her scattered wits and put down her drink.

"Well, uh, come on Stan," she said as she stood up. "Or we'll be late." She then remembered that she didn't even know where they were going for their date.

Back in the car, Stan directed Stacee to another house, where they were apparently going to visit a friend of his. As soon as they got there, Stacee headed to the bathroom and leaned against the locked door as she exhaled deeply. With her ears still ringing from Stan's surprising serenade, she knew that this was turning out to be a big mistake. All she needed was an excuse—some reason to walk out right now and drive home. But where was she going to find an excuse like that?

In fact the *excuse* found *her.* The moment she walked out of the bathroom.

Tan Stan the loud singing man and his buddy were sitting on the floor in a fog of sickly sweet marijuana smoke. Stan had just taken a big hit and was passing the bong back to his friend.

"I think this date is over," said Stacee as she fished her car keys from her purse and turned toward the door. But Stan didn't seem to hear her. . . .

Stacee Edwards still lives in Portland, but has found a new tanning salon. She believes that she has finally completely regained her hearing.

🔱 hey waiter! great buns!

Sometimes you meet someone and it's instant chemistry. That's what happened to Veronica. She was introduced to "Bud" at a party. They seemed to hit it off instantly, and spent the rest of the evening talking, almost oblivious to the other partygoers surrounding them.

Before the night was over, they made a date for the following weekend. Bud was a waiter, and he didn't own a car, so he gave Veronica an address and asked her to pick him up there.

It was a ninety-minute drive to the address Bud had given her, but she really didn't mind. Bud was a great-looking guy and seemed really nice, so who could say where this date might lead?

When Bud opened the door, she was surprised to find the living room filled with guys sitting around drinking beer. Bud grinned apologetically.

"I'm sorry, Veronica," he said. "We've been playing basketball, and we've only just got back. Grab a beer and relax while I take a shower. I'll just be a few minutes."

Won over by Bud's charm, she popped the top off a can of beer and parked herself in the middle of half a dozen sweaty guys watching a ballgame on television. After a while, she checked her watch. A little later she checked it again. Bud's "few minutes" was turning into nearly *forty-five* minutes. It had better be worth it.

It was. Veronica told us that Bud came bounding down the steps wearing a devilish smile and the best pair of butt-enhancing jeans she'd ever seen. Definitely worth the wait!

They went to a great little restaurant and enjoyed an intimate dinner. As he paid the check, Bud looked across at her with his lopsided smile.

"Let's not go back to my apartment," he said. "We'll go to the most romantic spot in town."

Of course, Veronica agreed. She handed over the car keys to Bud, who told her it was kind of hard to give directions so it would be easier if he drove. They drove ever higher along deserted rural roads, until he pulled into a tiny dirt road halfway up a mountain.

Veronica was a little taken aback. No gorgeous view, no romantic sunset. Just a gate and a sign that said "Park Closed for the Season." But that didn't matter. They ended up talking through the night. Bud was sweet, funny, adorable, and, *yes!* There was some serious chemistry here!

Before they knew it, the gray light of dawn was breaking. With a yawn, Bud suggested they head back to town and grab some breakfast. There wasn't time for him to get home and change before he went to work. Could Veronica drop him off after breakfast at the restaurant where he worked? No problem.

As Veronica pulled away from the restaurant with a final wave to Bud, she suddenly remembered that she'd left her purse back at Bud's apartment the previous evening. She looked at her watch. Surely one of Bud's housemates would be up by now. She'd swing by there before heading out to the freeway.

On the way to Bud's house, Veronica's mind replayed every romantic nuance of her date with Bud. He certainly was a wonderful guy. . . .

She knocked on the door, expecting it to be opened by a bleary-eyed guy in a rumpled basketball shirt. She was in for a surprise.

The door opened a few inches, revealing the face of a young blonde woman. Veronica explained that she'd left her purse here the previous evening. The young woman smiled.

"Yeah, I found it. You must be the girlfriend of one of Bud's friends. I'm Lila, Bud's fiancée. Come on in."

Lila pulled open the door, and Veronica got her second surprise. Lila was very obviously pregnant. Gathering her purse, her stomach, and her wits, Veronica somehow made it back to her car in a state of shock. She sat in her car for a few minutes, and the shock slowly turned to anger. Deciding to give this creep a piece of her mind, she peeled out from the curb and headed back to the restaurant.

Striding through the doors, she looked around and quickly spotted Bud. Walking up to him, she hissed, "I want to see you in private . . . *now!*"

For a moment, Bud looked puzzled, then his trademark grin spread across his face. "It can't wait, huh?" he said. "Okay, just give me a few minutes."

Veronica fumed in the restaurant lobby until one of Bud's coworkers approached her, barely concealing a leer. "You can meet Bud

Hey Waiter! Great Buns!

down the hallway," he said jerking his head toward the rear of the restaurant.

Veronica followed the directions along the hall, until she heard Bud's voice call out softly to her from a half open door. Pushing it open, she found herself in a large linen closet. She also saw Bud lounging against a pile of tablecloths. Wearing a shirt, his familiar smile, and nothing else.

She stared at him in angry silence. Everything she had planned to say to him froze on her lips. Obviously, he didn't get it. Then she noticed Bud's jeans hanging on a hook by the door. The jeans that had looked so good to her just a few hours before. She made up her mind.

Grabbing the jeans and flipping off the light switch in a single motion, Veronica stepped back into the hallway. She slammed the door behind her, leaving Bud in the dark—literally and metaphorically. Bundling the jeans under her arm, she was out of the restaurant, into her car, and heading for the freeway almost before she realized what she'd done.

As her car sped homeward, the anger slowly dissipated, and she felt her body relaxing as the tension slipped away with the miles. She looked down at the pair of jeans on the passenger seat and began to giggle. She was wondering how Bud was going to explain to his boss—and his fiancée—how he had managed to lose his pants on his break!

Whenever Veronica needs a laugh, she pictures Bud waiting tables wrapped in a tablecloth.

⚔ a date for life

to be honest, Tom couldn't believe his luck. Greta was absolutely gorgeous. Thick, wavy auburn hair framing a beautiful face that lit up often with her sparkling smile. Not to mention a figure that any movie star would be proud of. Tom didn't know much about fashion, but even he could see that her perfectly tailored navy blue suit and silk blouse didn't come from the kind of stores where he shopped.

They had literally bumped into each other at the supermarket one evening. Tom had turned into an aisle just as Greta was leaving it. They scrabbled on the floor picking up their dropped groceries while Tom apologized profusely. But Greta didn't seem to mind. In fact she seemed inclined to linger. They chatted for a few minutes, then she held out her exquisitely manicured hand and introduced herself.

Later, outside the store and still in a daze, Tom realized that somehow he had managed to secure a date with the lovely Greta. He had been so overwhelmed by her presence that he couldn't remember all the details. They'd talked. They'd laughed. And he'd come away with a lunch date for the following day. He couldn't even remember actually asking her, but he must have. Unless she'd asked him. It didn't matter. He was going to have lunch with Greta, and that was all that mattered.

He arrived a few minutes early at the restaurant and tried to appear nonchalant as he scanned the entrance for Greta. He still wasn't sure she'd show up. After all, he was just an ordinary kind of guy, and Greta was . . . well, *Greta*. He fiddled with his napkin and pushed the salt and pepper shakers around the starched white tablecloth with nervous fingers.

Then he saw her. She was standing in the restaurant foyer looking around the dining room. She was wearing an elegantly cut hunter green suit with a raincoat draped over her shoulders. She was carrying a soft leather briefcase. She must have come from some sort of meeting, thought Tom, who realized that he had no idea what Greta did for a living. Had she told him at the grocery store? He couldn't remember. He'd been so dazzled by her beauty that he hadn't remembered much of their actual conversation.

Tom stood up and Greta caught his eye. With a little wave and a big smile, Greta weaved her way through the busy restaurant toward him. Following her progress, a waiter almost dropped a loaded tray.

"I'm sorry I'm a little late," said Greta as Tom narrowly beat out another waiter for the privilege of holding out her chair. Tom assured her that her timing was perfect.

Waving away a menu, Greta told the waiter she'd just have the soup du jour and a house salad. She turned her magnetic smile back to Tom.

"That's all I want," she explained. "But you have whatever you feel like." Tom closed his menu and told the waiter that he'd have the same.

"Now," said Greta as the waiter departed, "Let's talk!" She leaned forward, her eyes searching Tom's face. "Tell me all about yourself!"

This date was going pretty darn well so far, thought Tom. Here he was, sitting at a table with the most beautiful woman in the restaurant. He was the envy of every man in the place, judging by the furtive glances that nearby male diners were shooting in Greta's direction when their own lunch companions weren't looking.

The soup arrived just as Greta was summarizing some of Tom's *curriculum vitae*. She was checking off the main points on her fingers.

"So, you're single," said Greta. "Never been married? No children? Okay!" She put her head on one side and narrowed her eyes, as she looked him over appraisingly. Tom was beginning to feel like a prize bull at a county fair auction. Not that he minded.

"Let's see," Greta said slowly, "You're about thirty, right? Non-smoker? Non-drinker? Health pretty good?"

Tom assured her that she was right on all counts. He was a little taken aback at Greta's forthright questioning, but he reasoned that young women today had to be very careful when entering into relationships. In any case, he'd have told her the combination to the safe at Fort Knox if he'd known it and she'd asked for it.

As the salad plates arrived, Greta leaned back in her chair and raised her eyebrows. "Now, let's talk about your needs," she smiled.

My needs?! thought Tom. You want to hear about my needs? He cleared his throat. Despite the soup, his lips felt unusually dry.

"My . . . my needs?"

A Date for Life

"Yes," said Greta, nodding encouragingly. "Presumably, you'll want to get married someday. Have kids. Send them to college. Retire. That sort of thing."

"Well, uh, that's certainly a possibility," said Tom hesitantly. "But isn't it a little early to be, uh, thinking that far ahead?" Tom was feeling a little lightheaded. Things were moving a little faster than he'd anticipated. At this rate, they'd be married by Saturday.

"That's where most people make their mistake," said Greta, shaking her head with a knowing smile. "You should be thinking about your future needs right now. Then, together, we can decide which life plan works best for you."

"Life plan . . . ?"

"Yes," nodded Greta. "As I mentioned yesterday, I like to work very closely with my clients to make sure they get exactly the right life insurance they need."

Tom's heart felt as if a steel clamp had suddenly locked onto it. *Life insurance?* Greta was pulling a notepad from her briefcase. Sensing a change in the atmosphere, she looked up at Tom with concern.

"You don't mind if I make a few notes do you?" She chuckled as a thought struck her. "After all, it's not like we're on a date, is it?"

No, Tom had to agree. It certainly wasn't.

Tom is a graphic designer. And he has quite enough life insurance, thank you.

BAD THINGS
COME IN
THREES

☍ nightmare in three acts

inda told us that she wasn't sure she could really call this a Date From Hell. Mainly because she didn't actually get to date anyone. So it was more like a dress rehearsal for a Date From Hell that never made it to Broadway.

Prologue. Linda hadn't dated since her divorce. At first, she hadn't felt ready for a relationship of any kind. Later, she realized that she wasn't going anywhere or doing anything that was likely to bring her into contact with any single men. If she was going to find some male companionship, Linda decided, she was going to have to do something about it.

Linda knew two young women who seemed to be experts on the singles scene. From their conversation, Laura knew that "Allie" and "Beth" made a practice of going out on the town every Friday night. They seemed to have this dating business down to a fine art, so when they suggested that Linda join them on one of their weekly jaunts, she decided that this was her chance to test the chilly waters of single life.

Act One. Friday evening began at an oh-so-chic mixer for corporate Gen-Xers on the move. "You never know at these things," advised Allie as they prepared to mingle. "Always a chance you'll meet a single guy with a good job." Then she and Beth plunged into the throng, leaving Linda to fend for herself.

Linda picked up a glass of lukewarm white wine, and the trained reporter in her observed the frantic mixing going on around her. Men and women were talking incessantly about their jobs, while barely concealing their disinterest in whatever the other party was saying. Business cards were fervently pressed on anyone who made eye-contact, while the card presser anxiously scanned the room for a more productive contact.

As if by telepathy, Allie and Beth returned simultaneously to the spot near the entrance where they'd left Linda, and from which she had barely moved. They, on the other hand, had worked the room like the experts they were, and both had reached the same conclusion. "Nothing here," said Allie. "Let's move on."

Act Two, Scene One. The drama then moved to Beth's car. The three young ladies climbed in and set off on the next part of their evening's adventure. Sitting in the back seat, Linda sincerely hoped that it would be a lot more interesting than the first part. Boy, she thought, I am really out of practice.

Beth slowed the car to a crawl as they approached a well-known nightspot. Allie and Beth scanned the parking lot for a few moments, ignoring the angry honks from the cars behind them. Then, in unison, they shook their heads, and Beth accelerated back into the traffic. A puzzled Linda looked out the rear window. What was wrong with that place?

A few minutes later, they slowed down again outside another nightclub. Once more, the cars behind had to wait while Allie and Beth gave the parking lot their expert once-over. After several seconds of intense scrutiny, Allie turned to Beth with eyebrows raised in a silent question. Beth considered for a moment, then came to a decision. With a soft "nope," she hit the gas. Just what the hell is going on here? thought Linda.

When the car slowed down again for Allie and Beth to peruse a third nightspot, Linda was ready to lean forward and bang their silly heads together. She watched as her companions scrutinized the landscape like Revenuers sniffing out moonshine in the Kentucky backwoods.

"Well?" pondered Beth.

"Seen better. But it'll do." replied Allie, with a resigned shrug.

"Hey, what is all this?" Linda asked. "What are you looking at?"

Allie turned around and gave Linda one of those condescending "oh, you are so naïve" looks.

"You can tell a lot about what a place is going to be like just by looking at the cars in the parking lot," she explained. "Not enough cars means the place is too empty. Too many 'bad' cars, you don't want to go there."

Sensing Linda's bewilderment as they got out of the car, Beth added, "We're looking for a place with a lot of 'good' cars. You know, Mercedes, Beamers. Too many Chevys and pickups, you give it a pass."

Act Two, Scene Two. Linda followed her friends into the dimly lit and noisy singles bar. She was beginning to wish she was home in her sweats sipping a cup of cocoa.

With the skill that comes from years of practice, Allie and Beth immediately fell into conversation with a couple of good-looking guys. On the other hand, Linda spent the next hour jammed into a booth with half a dozen plumbing-fixture salesmen who were in town for their annual convention. The sweats and cocoa were looking really good to Linda by now. Why didn't I bring my own car? she thought, as the tubby, red-faced man squashed next to her began yet another plumbing joke.

Act Three. Linda's dateless date night wasn't over yet. Alllie and Beth unclogged Linda from her plumbers, and they trolled a few more bars before winding up for a late supper in the bar of yet another popular nightspot.

Linda was sipping her now-routine glass of lukewarm white wine when she noticed the look on Allie's face. Allie was staring at a man who had just walked in with a sexy babe clinging to him. Beth leaned over and hissed in Linda's ear that the guy was Allie's recently discarded boyfriend. Allie stared at her ex. Her ex stared back at her. Linda stared at her feet. For a long time. Please, just get me out of this, prayed Linda to herself during the icy silence.

It was well past midnight when one of Beth's ex-boyfriends strolled in, and another thirty minutes of silent staring began.

Linda was tired. She was miserable. She was in a bar the name of which she didn't know and which she never wanted to visit again. As she drooped between her mute, staring companions, Linda made a firm and silent resolution NEVER to go bobbing for dates again.

Curtain.

Linda is a journalist. She writes a column for a leading daily newspaper, which has a parking lot that wouldn't even get a second look from Allie and Beth.

⚡ long distance revenge

a Date From Hell is one thing. But we have discovered that *Hell* hath no fury like a woman scorned—especially if she is scorned while dressed in evening wear.

Nigel lives in Cambridge, England. Jim, a friend, invited him to come with him to Newcastle for the weekend. Jim's girlfriend was a student at a university in Newcastle, and there was to be an end-of-term ball on the grounds of a beautiful and ancient castle that was close to the college. It would be a fancy affair, Jim said. Tuxedos, orchestras, and all-night partying. Newcastle is about 250 miles from Cambridge, but Nigel thought this sounded like a fun weekend, and quickly agreed.

Arriving in Newcastle and checking into a hotel that was close to the site of the Ball, Nigel and Jim carefully dressed themselves in their penguin suits in preparation for the long night ahead.

Not long after reaching the castle and joining the crowds heading for the various tents set up on the lush green lawns, Nigel became separated from Jim, who had headed for one of the temporary dance floors with his girlfriend. Nigel didn't mind. He picked up a drink at one of the bars and looked around at the crowds of partying students.

Then he saw her.

He was smitten by her beauty, and she was gazing back at him, apparently as interested in him as he was in her. He swallowed hard and, summoning all his courage, pushed through the crowd and introduced himself.

Her name was Evelyn. She smiled at him and graciously accepted his offer to buy her a drink. Before long, they were sitting together with a group of her friends. But they had eyes only for each other. Oblivious to the hubbub around them, they talked and joked and danced together, and after about an hour, they kissed for the first time. They exchanged phone numbers, and it was looking as if this was the start of something big.

This was certainly turning out to be a great evening for Nigel! But his tragic error was coming fast.

Evelyn excused herself to join the long line at the makeshift ladies' room on the other side of the lawn. Nigel stayed with the group of Evelyn's friends, which was where he made his first mistake.

One of Evelyn's female buddies apparently took a shine to Nigel too. With Evelyn out of the picture, she cuddled up to Nigel, and soon had her arms around him. Perhaps it was the wine. Perhaps it was the flattering realization that he was attractive to not one but *two* pretty young women. In any case, that's when he made his second mistake. He allowed her to give him a long passionate kiss. As he said, "Resistance was pointless!"

Of course, at that very moment, Evelyn returned to find her friend and Nigel in a fervent liplock. Understandably, Evelyn was less than happy, and made it clear that Nigel was no longer welcome to her company. Humbly, he slunk away, mentally kicking himself for his momentary lapse.

Back home in Cambridge, Nigel decided he really had to see Evelyn again, and fished out from his wallet the crumpled paper bearing Evelyn's phone number. He dialed the number, and after a couple of rings, Evelyn answered. What's more, she seemed pleased to hear from him. Emboldened by her friendly demeanor, he asked if he could see her again. He held his breath.

"Sure, that'd be great," said Evelyn. "Come up to Newcastle on Friday evening. We can go out somewhere."

Her flat was quite hard to find, she told him, so it would be best if he could just drive into central Newcastle, then call her again from a pay phone so she could come and meet him. Nigel quickly agreed to this arrangement. He hung up with a smile. It was going to work out all right after all!

After leaving work a few hours early on Friday afternoon, Nigel set off on the 250 mile drive north to Newcastle. Negotiating the tangled traffic on the crowded English roads was a hassle, but Nigel decided it was worth it to see Evelyn again. A few hours later, he was standing at a pay phone with a finger pressed to his free ear in an attempt to block out the noise of the early evening traffic roaring by.

His call was answered by a female voice. No, she said, she wasn't Evelyn; she was her flatmate. No, he couldn't speak to Evelyn right now. She was in Liverpool.

"Liverpool?" choked Nigel. Surely he had misheard!

No, he hadn't. "Yes, she's in Liverpool, visiting her mum and dad," said the helpful flatmate. "Well, if she's got a date with you she must

Long Distance Revenge

be on her way back, I expect."

She gave him Evelyn's parents' phone number. It was beginning to drizzle as Nigel entered a nearby shop to get a handful of change for the long-distance call. The drizzle had become a steady rain by the time he returned to his payphone on the street corner. He dialed the Liverpool number and fed a large number of coins into the slot with cold wet fingers. At least he could ask her dad what time she'd left.

"Left for Newcastle?" echoed her puzzled parent, after Nigel explained the reason for his call. "You've made a mistake, young man. She won't be going back there 'til Monday. She's staying here with us for the weekend. She's gone to the pub with some of her friends."

Nigel slowly replaced the receiver. The cold rain trickled down his neck. Nigel felt miserable. A bus rumbled through the puddle in the gutter beside the payphone, sending up a miniature tidal wave of greasy water. Nigel was miserable.

There he was, in the middle of Newcastle, 250 miles from home, and struck with the realization that he was never to see Evelyn again. And he knew his friends would never let him live this one down.

Evelyn had taken her time, but she had gotten her revenge. Long distance.

Nigel lives in Cambridge, and tries his hardest to avoid long distance romances.

⚡ the case of the disappearing pilot

$\int$usan was ready. The dinner was bubbling away in the oven. The candles were lit. The Christmas decorations were twinkling and the cozy fire was crackling in the hearth. The appetizing aromas wafting from the kitchen mingled with the scent of the freshly cut Christmas tree. Susan looked in the mirror. She had to admit it: she looked great. Only one thing was missing. . . .

Larry had persuaded Susan to let him come and spend Christmas with her. Now, for Susan this was a major step, because Christmas was a big deal for her. So she had to know: *Was he absolutely sure?*

You see, Susan had reason to be cautious. She and Larry had been dating for around eight months, and they had great times together, particularly because they shared an interest in horseback riding. Larry was a pilot, so naturally he was away often. But several times he would promise to call her in a day or so as he waved goodbye, and then he would disappear for days at a time.

Apparently there was another woman. In fact Larry admitted as much. It wasn't that he actually loved this former girlfriend. Far from it. She was dull, boring, and pitiful. He spent these times away from Susan, he said, trying to break up with this sad creature. He compared breaking up with her to "taking the family dog to the pound."

Understandably, after two of his disappearing acts Susan had told him, "Enough. Go back to the family dog."

But then the holiday season came around. And so did Larry's phone call. He'd gotten a lot of things resolved, including that ugly obsession with his former girlfriend, he told Susan.

He was reformed. Couldn't they spend Christmas together? Please? He could be there Christmas Eve.

That's when Susan asked him, "Are you absolutely sure?"

"Yes, absolutely," he promised. "Can't wait to see you," he added as they hung up. So on Christmas Eve, Susan waited. Later, she was to describe this "date" in three short sentences:

"Never called. Never showed up. Nothing."

Try as she might, Susan was unable to summon up enough Christmas spirit to forgive and forget any more. And who can blame her?

Did Susan ever hear from Larry again? Yes. About ten months later, he called and asked if she could ever consider taking him back. The answer, of course, was no. And, perhaps not surprisingly, he wound up marrying "the family dog."

Susan Freeman is the owner of a horse farm in Triune, Tennessee.

THE EASY HUNDRED-STEP GUIDE TO A GUARANTEED DATE FROM HELL

Step 97—*Don't Plan Anything*

Invite your date out to dinner, but don't make reservations. This is particularly important on those "special" days, such as Valentine's Day or New Year's Eve. This way, you can both stand in line at one restaurant after another, while you humiliate yourself before a string of stony-eyed Maitre d's. With any luck, it will be raining—or even snowing—by the time you drag your fuming date into your final stop: an all-night greasy spoon. You will be the last customers before the place is shut down by the health department. When you next attempt to see your date, you will be refused admittance by the hospital administration.

⚘ just the three of us

When Gaetane passed her sixtieth year, she probably thought her share of Dates From Hell was finally over. But she was to find that whoever—or whatever—it is that deals out the cards of dating fortune had one more joker in the pack, just for her.

Gaetane, a widow, likes to keep herself in shape and is still an attractive woman. She had met a man named Bob to whom she was attracted. They had met several times in a sort of accidentally-on-purpose way, and Gaetane was beginning to think she'd found her "dream prince." And when he asked her out for a dinner date, she was on cloud nine.

Unfortunately, the Saturday night in question coincided with the annual visit of Gaetane's friend Molly from New York. Gaetane considered asking Bob if they could postpone their dinner date to the following weekend, but frankly, she was worried that this would rebuff Bob, and she didn't want to risk anything that might spoil her chances with her "dream prince." And in any case, surely Molly wouldn't mind staying in on her own for just one evening, considering how important this was!

In fact, when she told Molly that Bob would be calling that evening, Molly couldn't have been more understanding.

"Of course, I'll want to meet him," insisted Molly. "You make him sound wonderful!"

On Saturday evening, Gaetane checked her makeup one last time in the hall mirror before opening the door. Her handsome prince smiled down at her. Then Gaetane noticed Bob's eyes widen as they focused on something over her shoulder.

She turned and gasped as she saw what Bob was looking at. It was Molly standing on the bottom stair, striking a pose with one hand on the banister. She was dressed to kill in a short, tight dress and high heels. She stepped forward, wafting a trail of musky perfume as she eased past Gaetane with her hand out.

"You must be Bob," breathed Molly. "Gae's told me so much about you!"

Bob took Molly's hand and grinned sheepishly as Gaetane stood by, watching her "friend" fluttering her eyelashes and pouring on the charm.

When it was time to leave for their dinner date, Bob turned to Molly. "We sure hate to leave you here all alone. Would you like to join us?" he inquired politely.

Molly's innocent eyes opened wide. "Oh, no. Surely you two would prefer to be alone. Well! If you insist." She beamed at Bob, ignoring Gaetane's steely stare.

At the restaurant, the three of them sat in a booth. Gaetane was careful to sit beside Bob, but of course, this put Molly on the other side of the table. And Molly scooted down the bench until she was sitting opposite Bob. Before long, Molly complained that her feet were cold. Slipping out of her shoes, she placed her stockinged feet in Bob's lap and asked him to massage them. Practically drooling, Bob was only too happy to oblige.

Throughout the evening, Molly continued to flirt shamelessly with Bob, while Gaetane was forced to sit and fume, virtually ignored by her dream prince.

When dinner was over Bob drove the two ladies home. He walked them into the house and Molly excused herself to "go powder my nose." With arms folded, Gaetane turned her cool glare on Bob.

"I think you'd better leave," she told him quietly. A shamefaced Bob didn't argue.

A few minutes later Molly reappeared. "Where's Bob?" she asked. Gaetane replied icily that Bob had had to leave.

"Gosh," said Molly, sweetly. "I hope I haven't done anything to upset you."

The next day, Molly returned to New York, never to return. Which was just fine as far as Gaetane was concerned.

Gaetane says she saw her dream prince in a different light after that night, and didn't go out with him again. Her prince, she says, had turned into Kermit the Frog. She was too polite to mention Miss Piggy.

🔱 three's a crowd

Phillipa found out that dating two different men can be fun, just as long as you don't make the mistake of dating both at precisely the same time.

She had been dating Rick during her college days on and off for a couple of years. Then she met Bud in an accounting class, and during those less-than-thrilling bookkeeping lessons, they discovered they liked each other's company.

Christmas break rolled around, and Bud told Phillipa that he was flying back to Virginia to spend the holidays with his family. He had a favor to ask. Would Phillipa pick him up at the airport on his return and drive him back to school? They attended a state university in a city about forty miles from the airport, so of course she readily agreed. After all, she thought, this would be an excellent opportunity to get to know each other better. Just the two of them, away from the classroom, away from the college, and . . . well, away from prying eyes.

Here's where it all hits the fan.

The appointed day arrived, and Phillipa picked up Bud at the airport and headed back toward school. The weather was wet and wintery, and a freezing drizzle was sprinkling as dusk fell. Phillipa was enjoying this time alone with Bud, and then she saw a familiar van pulled onto the shoulder ahead of them. Her heart sank as she realized it was Rick. There he was, standing by his disabled vehicle, staring straight back at her car as it approached him along the almost deserted highway!

Realizing that she had little choice, she pulled over behind the stalled van to pick up her sometime companion.

"Rick, this is Bud. Bud, this is Rick." And, she added to herself, Phillipa, this is goodbye.

Apparently, Rick had decided to go shopping, seeing as how Phillipa had told him she was going to be "busy" that day, and on the way home, the old van had finally breathed its last.

Needless to say, no one felt very festive, and all three of them rode back to town in silence, with Phillipa gripping the steering wheel in misery on what seemed like a very, very long drive.

Three's a Crowd

As Phillipa ruefully reflected, she had tried to work a little bit of harmless double dealing, but both deals fell through. She had to face the hard truth: "I got busted!"

"Phillipa" is now president of her own company, providing hair and make-up services to the film and television industry.

the end . . .
or is it?

"YOU THINK THAT'S A DATE FROM HELL? WAIT 'TIL YOU HEAR MINE. . . ."

Is that what you said after you read the stories in this book? *Okay. We're listening.*

Yes, we want to hear about your Date From Hell, or your Moment Made In Heaven. We are busy compiling the second volume of this book and we would love to include your story. Here's how it works:

Write down a few details about your Date From Hell (or Moment Made in Heaven). You can keep it quite brief, if you wish, as long as you include enough to let us know why it was Hellish—or Heavenly. Don't try to copy the style of the stories in the book. Just use your own words. We'll edit or rewrite the stories to fit the book's format.

Send us your story in one of the ways shown below. If your story is being considered for publication, we'll get back to you and request your permission to use it. At that time, you can decide if you want us to use your real name, just your first name, or you may ask us to create a pseudonym to protect your identity! We'll need to know your mailing address so we can contact you, but nobody else will ever see it, and of course, it will not be printed in the book!

Now, here's the really good part. If your story is selected for publication, we'll send you a *FREE* signed first edition of the book! And you'll be able to bask in the glory of having your name revered around the world as one who has looked a Date From Hell in the face and lived to tell the tale. (Unless, of course you don't let us use your real name. In which case you'll merely be able to point out "your" story to your friends, and they'll go, "yeah, right.")

So if you've had a Date From Hell (or a Moment Made in Heaven), tell us about it, and *you* could be the star of the next volume!

how to reach us

By regular mail:
Victoria Jackson & Mike Harris
"Dates From Hell"
P.O. Box 60393
Nashville, TN, 37064, USA

By e-mail:
dfhinfo@bt1.com

Via our web site:
www.datesfromhell.com

Thank you in advance for sending us your story for *Dates From Hell (And A Few Moments Made In Heaven) Volume Two!* We can't wait to see it!

℣ victoria jackson & mike harris